The Single-Minded Christian

Exposing and Eliminating Double-Mindedness in the
Christian Life

Timothy G. Baise

Renown Publishing

The Single-Minded Christian / Timothy G. Baise
ISBN-13: 978-1-945793-57-8
ISBN-10: 1-945793-57-0

This book is dedicated to the Homeless Angels mission and to all the laborers who are laboring with us.

All proceeds from the sale of this book will feed the hungry, clothe the needy, house the homeless, set free those in bondage, and provide love and hope to the brokenhearted.

Thank You, Father.

CONTENTS

The Cost of Being Double-Minded

Do you want to experience God's goodness and have your prayers answered on a regular basis? Of course you do. Everybody does. And every Bible-believing, Christ-following, God-fearing human being should receive all that the Bible promises, including wisdom, peace, joy, prosperity, health, protection, answered prayer, and so much more. The reality is that most Christians are not experiencing God at that level for one reason or another—and I am tired of it!

I am in the habit of drifting off to sleep while listening to the Bible through the Bible.is app on my phone. One night, I woke up suddenly as the word "*anything*" flashed in my soul like a lightning bolt. A bit startled, I looked at my phone to find I was in the book of James. I backed up a couple of verses and heard:

> *But when you ask, you must believe and not doubt,*
> *because the one who doubts is like a wave of the sea,*
> *blown and tossed by the wind. That person should not*
> *expect to receive* **anything** *from the Lord. Such a per-*
> *son is double-minded and unstable in all they do.*
> **—James 1:6–8** (NIV, emphasis mine)

There it went again—the word *anything* stunned me. That person should not expect to receive anything. Not *anything?*

Beyond that word, the description of this person as "double-minded" shook me to the core. It was this very fault—this double-minded trait—that James said was causing the person to miss God altogether.

I knew at that moment, deep down, that the problem of double-mindedness was worse than I ever could have imagined. I understood that it very well could be one of the main issues separating us from the promises of the Bible.

What does it mean to be double-minded? Webster defines it as being wavering or hypocritical.[1] The Greek word for double-minded is *dipsychos*—*dis* meaning "twice" and *psyche* meaning "mind."[2] James used it to describe someone who is divided in his interests or loyalties, wavering, uncertain, doubtful—someone who is, at best, undecided, or at worst, two-faced. These are not adjectives you would want to apply to yourself or your way of thinking, whether in business, in your marriage, or in dealing with family or friends. No wonder God drew a hard line in the sand here!

Double-mindedness is an enemy of faith. Perhaps more accurately, it's a faith-killer. And faith is, of course, essential to our relationship with God:

> *Without faith it is impossible to please God.*
> **—Hebrews 11:6a** *(NIV)*

Being double-minded is so serious, Jesus said in Matthew 12:25b, *"Every kingdom divided against itself is brought to desolation, and every city or house divided against itself will not stand."* Jesus makes it abundantly clear that division is extremely destructive.

You are the temple of the Holy Ghost, designed by the Master Architect to house God Himself. If you are divided in your interests and loyalties between the Word and the world, you won't "stand" either.

Don't get me wrong—you may stand on your physical feet until you depart planet Earth. However, *"our struggle is not against **flesh and blood**, but against the rulers, against the authorities, against the powers of this dark world and against the spiritual forces of evil in the heavenly realms"* (Ephesians 6:12 NIV, emphasis mine). The real battle takes place in the spiritual realm, and your eternal destiny is at stake. The only way you can stand before God is to put your trust in Jesus Christ and follow Him wholeheartedly.

If you are internally divided, it does not matter if your outward actions show undivided devotion to God. He knows and judges your heart (Luke 16:15, Acts 15:8).

The reality of this doesn't get any clearer than Jesus' interaction with the scribes and Pharisees, who had the appearance of being holy but were missing the internal mark. Jesus declared:

> *Woe to you, scribes and Pharisees, hypocrites! For you are like whitewashed tombs which indeed appear beautiful outwardly, but inside are full of dead men's bones and all uncleanness. Even so you also outwardly appear righteous to men, but inside you are full of hypocrisy and lawlessness.*
> *—Matthew 23:27–28*

To add one more level of sobering reality, in talking about His return, Jesus stated:

> *Many will say to Me on that day, "Lord, Lord, have we not prophesied in Your name, and done many wonders in Your name?" And then I will declare to them, "I never knew you; depart from Me, you who practice lawlessness!"*
> *—Matthew 7:22–23*

Both of these scriptural references clearly show that you can appear to be living what we would call a Christian lifestyle yet be so far from the Truth that it isn't even funny. I honestly believe there are more professing Christians living this way today than ever before.

It is possible to be double-minded while at church, praying, or singing worship songs—even in those moments when you tell yourself you're standing in faith as a believer! If you live a life of merely outward devotion and are unaware of the hypocrisy, you may be wondering why you're unable to have a growing relationship with God or why your prayers are going unanswered.

The book of James presents the remedy for the problem of internal division:

> *So let God work his will in you. Yell a loud no to the Devil and watch him scamper. Say a quiet yes to God and he'll be there in no time. Quit dabbling in sin. Purify your inner life. Quit playing the field. Hit bottom, and cry your eyes out. The fun and games are over. Get serious, really serious. Get down on your knees before the Master; it's the only way you'll get on your feet.*
>
> ***—James 4:7-10*** *(MSG)*

The Amplified Bible says it this way:

> *So submit to [the authority of] God. Resist the devil [stand firm against him] and he will flee from you. Come close to God [with a contrite heart] and He will come close to you. Wash your hands, you sinners; and purify your [unfaithful] hearts, you double-minded [people]. Be miserable and grieve and weep [over your sin]. Let your [foolish] laughter be turned to mourning and your [reckless] joy to gloom. Humble yourselves [with an attitude of repentance and insignificance] in the presence of the Lord, and He will exalt you [He will lift you up, He will give you purpose].*
>
> ***—James 4:7-10*** *(AMP)*

Here James made it plain that double-mindedness does not need to be an unbeatable obstacle. He clearly provides the answer, but a huge mistake I see many people make is that they move too quickly past the very first sentence and never submit fully to God. How can you expect to resist the devil without fail while leaving out the most important ingredient? *Submit to God!* Eliminating double-mindedness is only one single, solid, unwavering decision away—yet it still needs to be made!

In Psalm 15:1 (NIV), David asked, "*LORD, who may dwell in your sacred tent? Who may live on your Holy mountain?*" and then proceeded to answer those very questions. One part of the answer is "*he who keeps an oath even when it hurts, and does not change their mind.*"

Making the decision to go all-in, to submit fully to God, indeed has worldly consequences. However, in verse 5, David's answer concludes with this reassurance: "*He who does these things shall never be moved.*" Let's build our future on the immovable Rock!

Double-Mindedness in the Bible

Even godly men in the Bible sometimes lapsed into double-mindedness. John the Baptist is one such example. John baptized Jesus, and while Jesus was still praying, John saw heaven open up. The Holy Spirit descended upon the Savior "*in bodily form like a dove,*" and a voice from heaven declared, "*You are My beloved son; in You I am well pleased*" (Luke 3:21–22). Yet, when John was imprisoned and facing death, John sent two of his disciples to Jesus asking, "*Are You the Coming One, or do we look for another?*" (Matthew 11:2–3).

According to the Bible, John had been filled with the Holy Spirit since before he was born (Luke 1:15), had visions of Jesus before he ever met Him (John 1:32), baptized Christ, witnessed the Holy Spirit descend upon Him from heaven, and heard God the Father speak audibly (Luke 3:21–22). Yet John still fell prey to the deception of doubt while in prison. John was just as human as you and I, and this proves that it is possible to doubt even the things we see, taste, and touch with our own hands when God does not immediately respond to our prayers during a crisis.

Our firsthand revelation of God can go right down the drain when persecution or trials come. For this reason, we have stories like John the Baptist's in Scripture—to help build us up in advance and sustain us through life's difficulties. It is our job to know and meditate on all of these different accounts, and to remember the human frailties they expose, so we do not fall away from our faith in an attempt at self-preservation.

In this case, Jesus sent John's disciples back with encouraging words, and He went on to describe John as greater than any other prophet to the people He taught that day (Luke 7:28).

Then consider Peter. He witnessed countless miracles during his walk with Jesus. Moreover, he was the one who got out of the boat to walk on the water (Matthew 14:28–30). Peter told Jesus he would die with Him (Matthew 26:35).

Yet this same Peter eventually denied Jesus three times (Matthew 26:69–75)! Initially, he acted completely ignorant: "*I neither know nor understand what you are saying*" (Mark 14:68a). As those around Peter insisted that he knew Jesus, he grew angry and started cursing them out (Mark 14:68–71). When he faced opposition and danger, Peter fell short.

Thankfully, if you humbly seek God's will and way of life, and couple this submission with a determination to obey His will and follow His way, God promises to remember your successes and your faith, not your short-term failures and lapses of judgment. John and Peter are proof of God's grace and patience with our human frailty. Their examples ought to encourage us as we continue following Jesus.

Join the Fight!

At first, you may not consider double-mindedness a problem. Can it really be that dangerous to your spiritual health? But, like a frog in a heating kettle, you often don't recognize the results of your compromises until it's too late. You may allow many factors other than Scripture to influence your decisions and disrupt your prayers. Ultimately, this may rob you of your relationship with God. It may also prevent prayers from being answered or knowledge from being revealed, ultimately keeping you from experiencing peace, joy, prosperity, healing, and all that the Bible promises.

In this book, you will be challenged to examine different areas of your life where double-mindedness can and most certainly does creep in—so that you can eradicate it and its negative effects. And at the end of each chapter, you'll find workbook sections to help you begin exposing, overcoming, and eliminating specific areas of double-mindedness in your life. Then you can begin confidently expecting to receive the promises from God that come from being a single-minded Christian.

It's time to receive more. It's time to hear from God and receive His goodness fully. It's time to do away with double-mindedness and take your position as a servant of the Savior of mankind, the Creator of the universe, the King of kings. It's time to show the world that the blessings of Abraham, David, Solomon, Joseph, and others in the Bible are still accessible to us in our lives today!

CHAPTER ONE

A Double-Minded Heart

Have you ever seen a garden that's been neglected? Maybe, just maybe, you're like me and have neglected one yourself, so you're intimately familiar with what happens. Sure, you'll get some fruits and vegetables that first year, and in year two a few results will show. But, by and large, in that third year, you'll have a good-looking briar patch. It doesn't take long for the weeds in a neglected garden to take over completely.

Much the same, it really doesn't take long for the cares of the world to creep in and take over your heart, which is why you are commanded to *"guard your heart above all else"* (Proverbs 4:23 NLT).

A failure to protect your heart diligently and fiercely comes from not fully believing in, respecting, or even knowing the whole Truth. A follower of Christ should be motivated by reading God's Word because it's alive and powerful (Hebrews 4:12). Studying the Bible in its entirety should generate heat and momentum within your soul to become more Christlike every single day.

One who is double-minded will take Scripture and only apply the parts that are pleasing or positive. One who is double-minded will be motivated by the good news in the Bible while ignoring the more challenging passages.

What kind of person are you? Are you someone who accepts and respects and puts into practice *all* of the biblical truths? Or do you pick and choose the parts that you want to apply to your life?

Just Do It!

James 1:22 admonishes, "*But be doers of the word, and not hearers only, deceiving yourselves*" (ESV). No one can earn his or her salvation, but one can lose out on salvation by being a hearer only and not a doer. You cannot have faith and do nothing. If you try, you will be at odds within yourself and quite possibly living a deceived, double-minded life.

A freshwater fish cannot live in the ocean. Likewise, a true disciple cannot live in the world (John 15:19, John 17:14). You cannot call Christ "Lord" or profess to be Christian—"i.e., Christlike"—and then continue living like the world (Romans 12:2).

If you are like so many today who have heard and now believe in some variation of a once-saved-always-saved message, please stay with me and remain open-minded as I discuss several examples that clearly warn against complacency in your walk of faith.

Paul wrote, in Hebrews 2:1–3a (ESV):

Therefore we must pay much closer attention to what we have heard, lest we drift away from it. For since the message declared by angels proved to be reliable, and every transgression or disobedience received its just punishment, how shall we escape if we neglect such a great salvation?

This passage indicates that even if you started out strong in your faith, you can carelessly let the Word slip away like water through your fingers.

What way is there, then, of being saved from punishment if we neglect this great salvation? There is no other way, which is why understanding this warning is of utmost importance.

There is no area of life that, if neglected, doesn't cost you something. So, why do you suppose you can neglect your relationship with God and have it not cost you everything? Neglect will ruin a man physically, financially, and spiritually.

Christ talked of misguided people whose lives are not built on the rock:

*Therefore everyone who hears these words of mine and puts them into practice is like a wise man who built his house on the rock. The rain came down, the streams rose, and the winds blew and beat against that house; yet it did not fall, because it had its foundation on the rock. But everyone who hears these words of mine and **does not** put them into practice is like a foolish man who built his house on sand. The* *rain came down, the streams rose, and the winds blew and beat against that house, and it fell with a great crash.*

—**Matthew 7:24–27**(NIV, emphasis mine)

The Bible is clear here. Wise people put God's Word into practice and are immovable in the face of adversity. They accept the challenging parts of the Bible as well as the good news. Foolish people may talk a good game, and may appear good on the outside, yet fail to do good works (Ephesians 2:10, 2 Timothy 3:17, Titus 2:14).

First John 3:18 (NLT) says, *"Let's not merely say that we love each other; let us show the truth by our actions."*

Jesus Himself stated, according to John 15:1–6 (NIV):

*I am the true vine, and my Father is the gardener. He cuts off every branch in me that bears no fruit, while every branch that does bear fruit he prunes so that it will be even more fruitful. You are already clean because of the word I have spoken to you. Remain in me, as I also remain in you. No branch can bear fruit by itself; it must remain in the vine. Neither can you bear fruit unless you remain in me. I am the vine; you are the branches. **If you remain in me** and I in you, you will bear much fruit; apart from me you can do nothing. **If you do not remain in me**, you are like a branch that is thrown away and withers; such branches are picked up, thrown into the fire and burned.* (emphasis mine)

The branches that do not bear fruit are cut off, thrown into the fire, and burned. That is a sobering thought, but it is reality. This verse absolutely shows that the branch (or people) described were "in Him"—connected, if you will—at one point, yet they yielded no fruit and, so, were cut off.

If is a big two-letter word, especially when an "*If you do*" and an "*If you do not*" statement appear side by side, as in this passage. You have a choice to stay in Him or not—but that choice is yours, not His! Your free will was not taken away the moment you were led through a sinner's prayer.

As you are pondering this thought, consider Paul's warning to us in Romans 11:17–22:

> *And if some of the branches were broken off, and you, being a wild olive tree, were grafted in among them, and with them became a partaker of the root and the fatness of the olive tree, do not boast against the branches. But if you do boast, remember that you do not support the root, but the root supports you.*
>
> *You will say then, "Branches were broken off that I might be grafted in." Well said. Because of unbelief they were broken off, and you stand by faith. Do not be haughty, but fear. For if God did not spare the natural branches, He may not spare you either. Therefore consider the goodness and severity of God: on those who fell, severity, but toward you, goodness,* **if you continue in His goodness.** *Otherwise you also will be cut off. (emphasis mine)*

If Jesus' finished work on the cross was as many believe today, then the Bible should only read as follows:

Old Testament, Matthew, Mark, Luke, John, Romans 10:9, add in a sinner's prayer, and amen!

Seriously, why would ninety percent of the New Testament writings ever need to have been recorded in Scripture if that were the case? Why would the vast majority of the New Testament contain warnings, rebukes, exhortations, commands, and demands to live a holy life if none of that really matters?

You cannot ignore what Jesus, Peter, Paul, James, and a whole host of other New Testament writers expressed. You cannot pick and choose the best-feeling parts of Scripture and have those alone apply to you, leaving out other, not-so-convenient, challenging, and hard-to-understand parts.

You have the choice. Either you go all-in with God or you risk losing everything.

Your Choice

This tendency to accept and be obedient to only part of God's Word while rejecting other parts of it is the first and most important area of double-mindedness that needs to be dealt with.

You must fully accept all of Scripture and God's commands before you will be able to tackle other areas of double-mindedness. You simply will not see victory until you take this important first step and open yourself up to the truth of the Word.

Read it. Study it—even the parts that are uncomfortable or seemingly outdated. God's Word is God's plan, and you are either on board with it completely or you're not.

You will either obey His commands and do what He asks or you won't. There is no compromise here. There is no meeting God halfway. Either you're in or you're out.

Matthew 25:31–46 beautifully illustrates the importance of obedience to Scripture. This passage describes how Jesus will judge the nations based on whether or not they have obeyed God's commands to show mercy and justice to marginalized persons:

When the Son of Man comes in His glory, and all the holy angels with Him, then He will sit on the throne of His glory. All the nations will be gathered before Him, and He will separate them one from another, as a shepherd divides his sheep from the goats. And He will set the sheep on His right hand, "Come, you blessed of My Father, inherit the kingdom prepared for you from the foundation of the world: for I was hungry and you gave Me food; I was thirsty and you gave Me drink; I was a stranger and you took Me in; I was naked and you clothed Me; I was sick and you visited Me, I was in prison and you came to Me."

Then the righteous will answer Him, saying, "Lord, when did we see You hungry and feed You, or thirsty and give You drink? When did we see You a stranger and take You in, or naked and clothe You? Or when did we see You sick, or in prison, and come to You?" And the king will answer and say to them, "Assuredly, I say to you, inasmuch as you did it to one of the least of these My brethren, you did it to Me."

Then He will also say to those on the left hand, "Depart from me, you cursed, into the everlasting fire prepared for the devil and his angels: for I was hungry and you gave Me no food; I was thirsty and you gave Me no drink; I was a stranger and you did not take Me in, naked and you did not clothe Me, sick and in prison and you did not visit Me."

Then they also will answer Him, saying, "Lord, when did we see you hungry or thirsty or a stranger or naked or sick or in prison, and did not minister to You?" Then He will answer them, saying, "Assuredly, I say to you, inasmuch as you did not do it to one of the least of these, you did not do it to Me." And these will go away into everlasting punishment, but the righteous into eternal life.

As Christians, we are called to help those in need. The Bible makes it abundantly clear how seriously God takes these matters of social justice: they are not optional or open to discussion. We are not saved by our obedience, but our obedience makes our faith alive as we look to experience God's perfect, saving grace.

A Firm Foundation

Many professing Christians really have no clue what the Bible says or doesn't say, and they certainly don't know how to apply it in their lives. They are merely drifting along in life. They are prey to the enemy and the forces of this world.

Other Christians know what the Bible says, but they only pay attention to the parts that are convenient. They ignore God's voice asking them to step out in faith, and they skip over the commands that don't agree with their lifestyle.

And then, some Christians understand the importance of accepting all of God's Word. They strive to do what He asks at all times, and they believe wholeheartedly in Him.

The first two categories lead to ignorance and double-mindedness. The last leads to a full life in Christ, to receiving all of His promises and blessings.

Strive to be a doer of God's Word, not just a hearer (James 1:22). Open up your heart to all of His truth. Don't pick and choose what works for you. Being a doer of His Word requires a selfless sacrifice but will bring you great reward.

WORKBOOK

Chapter One Questions

Question: What are some passages of Scripture that you find especially difficult or challenging? Is the trouble from insufficient understanding of the passage or because obeying it is difficult, inconvenient, or countercultural?

_____

_____

_____

_____

_____

_____

_____

_____

_____

Question: What are some well-known scriptures that even non-Christians are generally familiar with and appreciate? What are some parts of the Bible that cause unbelievers to scoff or rebel? What are some passages that Christian circles love? What are some that are rarely addressed?

_____

_____

_____

_____

_____

_____

_____

_____

_____

_____

_____

_____

Question: What differentiates a passage that _does not apply_ to the church (e.g., Old Testament sacrificial system) from a passage that _is not being applied_ in the church because of double-mindedness?

_____

_____

_____

_____

_____

_____

_____

_____

_____

_____

_____

Action: Have you read *all* of the Bible? Do you read it *all* regularly? Commit to being a student of all Scripture. Download the Bible.is app today and begin listening to the Bible every single day.

Chapter One Notes

_____

_____

_____

_____

_____

_____

_____

_____

_____

_____

_____

_____

_____

_____

_____

_____

_____

_____

_____

_____

CHAPTER TWO

A Double-Minded Tongue

I believe that the devil himself concocted the taunt: "Sticks and stones can break my bones, but words will never hurt me." What a flat-out lie to teach kids so early in life! We all soon learn that words can hurt much more, with way more extensive consequences, yet we continue to hand down this lie from generation to generation.

Countless books have been written on the power of the tongue. My goal with this book, however, is simple: to expose the double-mindedness within the words and attitudes that come from our speech. The best way for me to open this up is with James 3:9–12:

With it we bless our God and Father, and with it we curse men, who have been made in the similitude of God. Out of the same mouth proceed blessing and cursing. My brethren, these things ought not to be so. Does a spring send forth fresh water and bitter from the same opening? Can a fig tree, my brethren, bear olives, or a grapevine bear figs?

I mean seriously, these are great questions! Can a drinking fountain send forth both fresh and salt water simultaneously? Not a chance! When was the last time you went to an apple orchard and were able to pick pineapples? Never.

That's because either of these occurrences would go against the nature of God's creation. How, then, can a man or woman of God, having a new nature, say good things about God in one moment but gossip, complain, curse, and even hate their neighbor a moment later? Herein lies the unrelenting, deceptive double-mindedness that plagues so many believers.

The Bible is not silent on the topic of the tongue and the devastation that can be brought about through the words we say. Scripture after scripture addresses the problem of the dangerous nature of the tongue:

Those that consider themselves religious and yet do not keep a tight rein on their tongues deceive themselves, and their religion is worthless.
—James 1:26 (NIV)

Let no corrupt word proceed out of your mouth, but what is good for necessary edification, that it may impart grace to the hearers.
—Ephesians 4:29

But now you yourselves are to put off all these: anger, wrath, malice, blasphemy, filthy language out of your mouth.

—Colossians 3:8

He who would love life and see good days, let him refrain his tongue from evil, and his lips from speaking deceit.

—1 Peter 3:10

Keep your tongue from evil, and your lips from speaking deceit.

—Psalm 34:13

A wholesome tongue is a tree of life, but perverseness in it breaks the spirit.

—Proverbs 15:4

I could provide so many more Scripture references, but I think I've proven the point. A man or woman of God should never use his or her tongue to produce deception, to curse, to tear down, to gossip, to lie, to murmur, or to complain. Yet these are areas in which our double-mindedness tries to fool us.

Words of the Heart

As Christians, we are to love our neighbor, yet too often, the things we say communicate the exact opposite. Proverbs 18:21a states: *"Death and life are in the power of the tongue."* You communicate death or life by what you say! Your words can have the best or absolute worst impact on another's life. Your words can scar a person more deeply than any paddle on the backside or punch in the face.

Not only can your words scar the people whom God has called you to love, but they also reveal what is truly in your heart. According to Luke 6:45 (NIV), *"A good man brings good things out of the good stored up in his heart, and an evil man brings evil things out of the evil stored up in his heart. For the mouth speaks what the heart is full of."*

In the same vein, James 3:12a states, *"Can a fig tree, my brethren, bear olives, or a grapevine bear figs?"* If your heart is full of love, joy, peace, long-suffering, kindness, goodness, gentleness, faithfulness, and self-control (Galatians 5:22–23a), then those qualities will come forth in the words you use. If your heart is full of impurity, enmity, strife, jealousy, anger, rivalries, dissensions, division, or envy, then *those* things will be revealed in your speech (Galatians 5:19–21).

Controlling the Tongue

In addition to seeking God and asking Him to settle your heart and your speech, here are some questions you can ask yourself to help rid your life of the double-minded tongue:

- Does this need to be said, or do I just want to say it?

- Will my words build up or tear down?

- Will my words help or hurt someone?

- Are my thoughts and words selfishly motivated, or are they born out of love and compassion for others?

Speaking words that build up and encourage brings life, but speaking words that tear down, overwhelm, and depress *"crushes the spirit"* (Proverbs 15:4 NIV)—and it really hurts you in the long run. As Jesus warned, *"I say to you that for every idle word men may speak, they will give account of it in the day of judgment. For by your words you will be justified, and by your words you will be condemned"* (Matthew 12:36–37).

Therefore, guard your tongue carefully and avoid being double-minded in your speech. Seek to speak words of life to build up believers in the Lord and to share the good news of Jesus Christ with those who don't know Him yet.

And remember that problems of the tongue are ultimately problems of the heart. Ask God to change and purify *your* heart so that your words will be pleasing to Him.

WORKBOOK

Chapter Two Questions

Question: When was the most recent time you used your tongue to bless God? When was the most recent time you used it to curse man? If being double-minded in your speech is a problem for you, what is one step you can take toward eliminating the problem?

_____

_____

_____

_____

_____

_____

_____

_____

Question: List words that describe godly, edifying speech and those that describe ungodly, destructive speech.

_____

_____

_____

_____

_____

_____

_____

_____

_____

Question: Recall a time when someone's words brought life and healing. When did someone's words tear you down? When have your words affected others in these ways?

_____

_____

_____

_____

_____

_____

_____

_____

_____

_____

Action: Evaluate the comments you have made on social media using the four questions at the end of this chapter. Write these questions out and put them where they will remind you to think before you post.

Chapter Two Notes

CHAPTER THREE

Double-Minded Favoritism

The next time you're at church, take a look around. You'll see many families seated together, but look closely at the groups of friends who are seated in the sanctuary. Chances are they look a lot alike. They are probably of the same race, the same age, and similar socioeconomic status.

This is not something unique to churches. In schools, prisons, workplaces, and other venues, people gravitate toward those who are similar to them.[3] We do this because it's comfortable.

Would you believe that this, too, can be an area of double-mindedness?

Showing Favoritism

Preferring one type of person over another is a form of favoritism. One definition says that favoritism is "the unfair practice of treating some people better than others."[4] Another describes it as "a display of partiality toward a favored person or group."[5] Some synonyms include *partiality*, *discrimination*, and *preference*. The Greek word for favoritism is *prosopolempsia*, which means partiality or, more fully defined, "the fault of one who when called on to give judgement has respect of the outward circumstance of man and not to their intrinsic merits, and so prefers, as the more worthy, one who is rich, high born, or powerful, to another who does not have these qualities."[6]

God does not show favoritism. Scripture tells us that *"there is no partiality with God"* (Romans 2:11).

If God had shown favoritism, He would have died only for the Jews! Instead, God welcomes all people and is comfortable with all people. He judges everyone the same way:

And if you call on the Father, who without partiality judges according to each one's work, conduct yourselves throughout the time of your stay here in fear.
—1 Peter 1:17

Then Peter opened his mouth and said: "In truth I perceive that God shows no partiality.
—Acts 10:34

We are all created equal under heaven, made in God's likeness and image, designed for fellowship and unity with our Creator. If you hold to the Christian standard and fly the Christian flag, if you say you are in Him and abide in Him—without which there is no hope—then you ought to walk as He walked (1 John 2:6).

Partiality can hinder your relationship with God and shut down your prayer life. It may be stopping you from receiving a blessing. It could be allowing the devil to reign in your life, creating poverty, sickness, fear, and worry—and the list goes on. Partiality can cripple your understanding and prevent you from growing into the man or woman God intended you to be.

James starts chapter 2 with these words: "*My dear brothers and sisters, how can you claim to have faith in our glorious Lord Jesus Christ if you favor some people over others?*" (NLT). You can read through a variety of other translations and see that he is basically saying it's impossible to hold to the faith in Christ while despising His creation.

Whoever claims to love God yet hates a brother or sister is a liar. For whoever does not love their brother and sister, whom they have seen, cannot love God, whom they have not seen. And he has given us this command: Anyone who loves God must also love their brother and sister.
—1 John 4:20–21(NIV)

Loving God translates into loving the people He has made, even if they are not like us and we cannot relate to them. Outward appearance and social or financial standing are irrelevant to God, so we cannot judge others by these standards. Instead, we ought to show Christ's love with the same impartiality He showed when He died for us while we were still sinners (Romans 5:8).

Church Cliques

Unfortunately, partiality isn't a new problem in the church. People in the early church were already biased toward people they liked or those they thought could give them something. Biased fellowship creates division in the body. It is a violation of the command given in Leviticus: *"...but you shall love your neighbor as yourself"* (Leviticus 19:18).

This issue of partiality was prevalent enough during His earthly ministry that Jesus told the story of the Good Samaritan to His followers (Luke 10:25–37). Jesus caused heads to turn when He interacted with prostitutes, tax collectors, Samaritans, and any other sinner who came to Him. In the days of the early church, He sent Paul to minister to the Gentiles (Acts 9:15).

Unlike Paul, Peter struggled with partiality. Peter had no problem socializing with Gentiles when no one was looking, but the moment other Jewish folks showed up, he immediately shunned those in his presence for fear of what they might think. He was ultimately reprimanded for his hypocritical, two-faced fellowship that caused so many others to stumble (Galatians 2:11–21).

Jesus was adamant about breaking the sin of favoritism, and His disciples generally caught on. James wrote: *"If you really keep the royal law found in Scripture, 'Love your neighbor as yourself,' you are doing right. But if you show favoritism, you sin and are convicted by the law as lawbreakers"* (James 2:8–9 NIV). Favoritism is a serious offense against God's call to love.

Love Really Does Win

Remember, Scripture says love is the *"fulfilling of the law"* (Romans 13:10, Galatians 5:14), *"drives out fear"* (1 John 4:18 NIV), *"covers a multitude of sin"* (1 Peter 4:8 NIV), provides protection from judgment in Christ (Psalm 91:14–16), and *"never fails"* (1 Corinthians 13:4–8).

You might struggle with double-minded favoritism, but the good news is that the best way to rid your life of it is to love everyone, including those who are different from you.

The next time you go to church, find someone less fortunate (or more fortunate) to talk to. Sit with someone who doesn't look like you. Invite someone with a different viewpoint or different background over for dinner. Do this at church, and then do it at work, in your neighborhood, and at the gym.

Be radical and let them see your light!

WORKBOOK

Chapter Three Questions

Question: Toward what types of people are you inclined to show favoritism? What types of people are you most likely to avoid? Consider both external and internal factors (economic status, nationality, race, marital status, political affiliation, family dynamics, educational background, employment type, personal appearance, etc.).

_____

_____

_____

_____

_____

_____

_____

_____

_____

Question: How does showing favoritism violate God's commands and offend His character?

_____

_____

_____

_____

_____

_____

_____

_____

_____

Question: Have you been on the receiving end of discrimination or cliquishness? How did it affect you? When might you have treated others similarly (in a different context)?

_____

_____

_____

_____

_____

_____

_____

_____

_____

_____

_____

Action: How often do you interact with people who are not like you? What are some ways you could intentionally do so? Write out a list and choose two to three to implement this week.

_____

_____

_____

_____

_____

_____

_____

_____

_____

Chapter Three Notes

CHAPTER FOUR

A Double-Minded Knowledge of God

Children love dressing up as their favorite superheroes. They put on a cape and run around the house, pretending to accomplish feats of strength and daring rescues. In those moments, they believe they are greater than they were before, and it affects everything about them, from the way they interact with others to the way they solve problems.

As Christians, we have much more than a mere superhero cape to put on daily: we are to *"put on the Lord Jesus Christ"* (Romans 13:14). Paul said you must *"put on the whole armor of God"* (Ephesians 6:10–17). This armor is for your well-being and your ability to withstand the devil and his deceptive lies. Thus equipped, you can endure his wickedness, treachery, hardships, sickness, evil, and malicious acts in your life—whatever he throws at you.

However, putting on Christ as Lord, Savior, Healer, Provider, and Protector does not mean that you can stow

Him in the closet for a rainy day. Wear Him with childlike faith, like a five-year-old in a costume with a cape! A double-minded person is incapable of putting on the whole armor of God. Such a person may be able to swing the sword occasionally, yet he or she will ultimately fall short.

If you want to be single-minded, you need to rest in a deep knowledge of God that is rooted in Scripture. You need to truly know God, trusting that He does not change (Malachi 3:6) and that His promises are always true (2 Corinthians 1:20).

Knowing God

It's possible to be double-minded about God's nature, His character, His mercy, His loving-kindness, or even His thoughts. James addressed the fact that some were blaming God for their misfortunes, heartaches, sickness, and other worldly distractions. Many today are unsure whether or not something is in God's will.

You might think a hardship or struggle is some test from God to correct or shape you. Again, this is mostly a problem of not knowing what the Bible says in the first place. God does not create trouble in your life! James 1:12–17 declares:

> *Blessed is the man who endures temptation; for when he has been approved, he will receive the crown of life which the Lord has promised to those who love Him. Let no one say when he is tempted, 'I am tempted by God'; for God cannot be tempted by evil, nor does He Himself tempt anyone. But each one is tempted when he is drawn away by his own desires and enticed.*

Then, when desire has conceived, it gives birth to sin; and sin, when it is full-grown, brings forth death.

Do not be deceived, my beloved brethren. Every good gift and every perfect gift is from above, and comes down from the Father of lights, with whom there is no variation or shadow of turning.

No variance. None. This does not mean that God is good 99.999 percent of the time and there is still a 0.001 percent chance that He might be bad. It boggles my mind that anyone could read this verse and still believe that God puts trouble on people.

If this doesn't convince you, read John 10:10: *"The thief does not come except to steal, and to kill, and to destroy. I have come that they may have life, and that they may have it more abundantly."*

Or, as 1 Corinthians 10:13 (ESV) tells us:

No temptation has overtaken you that is not common to man. God is faithful, and he will not let you be tempted beyond your ability, but with the temptation he will also provide the way of escape, that you may be able to endure it.

It seems to me that any type of blame game to avoid taking personal responsibility is a deception that comes from our own hearts. Scripture does not say that you won't be tempted or tested. It clearly says that you will. However, these trials are not from God.

God goes before you to make sure that at every crazy turn you take, every dumb decision you make, He has a plan for your life that brings you back to Him. Check out a select few verses that clearly communicate God's goodness:

Oh, taste and see that the LORD is good; blessed is the man who trusts in Him!
—Psalm 34:8

The LORD is good, a stronghold in the day of trouble; and He knows those who trust in Him.
—Nahum 1:7

For the LORD your God is gracious and merciful, and will not turn His face from you if you return to Him.
—2 Chronicles 30:9b

For the LORD God is a sun and shield; the LORD will give grace and glory. No good thing will He withhold from those who walk uprightly.
—Psalm 84:11

If you then, being evil, know how to give good gifts to your children, how much more will your Father who is in heaven give good things to those who ask Him!
—Matthew 7:11

And we know that all things work together for good to those who love God, to those who are the called according to His purpose.

—Romans 8:28

...God anointed Jesus of Nazareth with the Holy Spirit and with power, who went about doing good and healing all who were oppressed by the devil, for God was with him.

—Acts 10:38

Every good gift and every perfect gift is from above, and comes down from the Father of lights, with whom there is no variation or shadow of turning.

—James 1:17

Best of all, He promises never to leave you or forsake you (Hebrews 13:5).

No matter what the situation, no matter how big the trouble, no matter how bad it looks, there is a *"way of escape"*! You need to quit wallowing around in the circumstances of life and start looking for and trusting in His way.

WORKBOOK

Chapter Four Questions

Question: Have you ever doubted God's goodness when you were going through a difficult time? What is the source of evil and trouble?

_____

_____

_____

_____

_____

_____

_____

_____

_____

_____

_____

Question: What are the different names given to God in the Bible? What does each name represent? How does knowing each of these names refine your perspective on His character?

_____

_____

_____

_____

_____

_____

_____

_____

_____

_____

Question: What is the difference between being double-minded and living in balance?

_____

_____

_____

_____

_____

_____

_____

_____

_____

_____

_____

_____

Action: Study Ephesians 6 regarding the armor of God that Christians are to put on. What is the significance of each piece? Where in the Bible does God say He will be your rear guard?

_____

_____

_____

_____

_____

_____

_____

_____

_____

_____

_____

Chapter Four Notes

_____

_____

_____

_____

_____

_____

_____

_____

_____

_____

_____

_____

_____

_____

_____

_____

_____

_____

_____

_____

_____

_____

CHAPTER FIVE

A Double-Minded View of Sin

Luke 7:36–50 records an encounter between Jesus and a sinful woman who washed His feet at the home of a Pharisee named Simon, who was appalled by the fact that Jesus let this woman touch Him.

Jesus, knowing what was in Simon's heart, initiated a conversation with him and told him the following parable:

> *"There was a certain creditor who had two debtors. One owed five hundred denarii, and the other fifty. And when they had nothing with which to repay, he freely forgave them both. Tell Me, therefore, which of them will love him more?"*
>
> *Simon answered and said, "I suppose the one whom he forgave more."*
>
> *And He said to him, "You have rightly judged." Then He turned to the woman and said to Simon, "Do you see this woman? I entered your house; you gave Me no water for My feet, but she has washed My feet with*

her tears and wiped them with the hair of her head.
You gave Me no kiss, but this woman has not ceased
to kiss My feet since the time I came in. You did not
anoint My head with oil, but this woman has anointed
My feet with fragrant oil. Therefore I say to you, her
sins, which are many, are forgiven, for she loved
much. But to whom little is forgiven, the same loves
little."

—Luke 7:41–47

Simon clearly did not realize how bad his own personal condition was. Unlike the woman, he was prideful and did not think of himself as a sinner. He was probably resting in his high social status as a Pharisee and did not understand that, like the woman, he was also falling short of keeping the law perfectly.

It is easy for us to judge the self-righteousness of the Pharisees, but many Christians today are guilty of the same attitude of feeling superior to others whom they consider to be more sinful or whose sins they consider to be more severe.

A Love That Covers Sin

According to Jesus, if you don't understand how much you've been forgiven, you will not be able to fulfill God's command to *"love the LORD your God with all your heart, with all your soul, and with all your mind"* and to *"love your neighbor as yourself"* (Matthew 22:37–39). Rather, you will only have the capacity to *"love little."*

To truly love God, we have to understand who He is and what He has done for us. We have to be aware of the severity of the sin that separated us from Him—from which He saved us at the cost of His own life. If we can grasp this great sacrificial love and the depth of our own sin, we can extend love to others rather than judge them as being worse than we are. If we believe only for a second that we could be saved by our own merits, we are living a lie.

James 2:10 shows that if you were to keep the whole law and yet stumble at just one point, you would be guilty of breaking it all. In other words, you could be the best role model on earth, having kept yourself from all the major no-no's and attended church every Sunday for forty years, but the moment you tell one single lie, in spiritual terms—to God—it's as if you are a lying, drunk, adulterous, idol-worshipping, blasphemous murderer in need of forgiveness and reconciliation.

This lines up perfectly with what God told Adam in the garden: "...*in the day you eat of [the fruit] you shall surely die*" (Genesis 2:17b). Adam disobeyed in one detail but was immediately found guilty of the entire fall of mankind, and that disobedience brought spiritual death. Spiritual death brings separation from God, guilt, condemnation, fear, blame, deceit, strife, sorrow, pain, sickness, hard work, poverty, and physical death.

Romans 5:20a says that God's law "*was brought in that the offense might abound.*" In other words, the law brought attention to sin and made a big deal out of it.

This is why 1 Corinthians 15:56b states that "*the strength of sin is the law.*" The law was added so sin would take on the characteristic of transgressions, the consciousness of sin would be intensified, and the desire for redemption would be aroused. In essence, the law was paving the way to a Savior.

Jesus said in Matthew 5:17, "*I did not come to destroy [the law] but to fulfil [it]*." He came to fulfill the law because we couldn't do it out of our own ability, no matter how hard we tried. Jesus did not take the law away, but He gave us the answer to the toughest test man would ever have to take, and that answer is love.

According to Romans 13:10, "*Love does no harm to a neighbor; therefore love is the fulfillment of the law.*" In the same vein, 1 Peter 4:8b states that "*love will cover a multitude of sins.*" Anytime you are not operating in love, you are defiantly acting out in disobedience to the command of Christ, just as Adam did in the garden. You allow yourself to be separated from God; you allow guilt, condemnation, fear, blame, deceit, strife, sorrow, pain, sickness, hard work, poverty, and physical death to come into your life.

The penalty of just one sin carries the weight of all sin, and when you commit to following Christ and turn in repentance from your old ways, the blood sacrifice He made on the cross covers it all.

You must know, recognize, and understand your spiritual condition for what it really is in order to humble yourself properly and follow His example to love others sacrificially.

Selective Obedience

James 2:8–11 puts it this way:

> *If you really fulfill the royal law according to the Scripture, "You shall love your neighbor as yourself," you do well; but if you show partiality, you commit sin, and are convicted by the law as transgressors.* <u>*For whoever shall keep the whole law, and yet stumble in one point, he is guilty of all.*</u> *For He who said, "Do not commit adultery," also said, "Do not murder." Now if you do not commit adultery, but you do murder, you have become a transgressor of the law.*

You are wrong if you think that keeping one law, or refraining from certain bad things, earns more favor from God than keeping another. There is no difference in the weight of sin. If you stumble in just one point, which we all have done, it's as if you are a lying, drunk, adulterous, idol-worshipping murderer!

Unfortunately, today, the vast majority of people have been tainted by society and the laws of the land. We have been programmed to believe that certain violations are worse than others.

When standing in a grocery store line, most people wouldn't dare pocket an item, even as small as a pack of gum. However, many of those same people, whom we would consider "good," have no problem stealing something of far greater value, day in and day out: time.

You see, stealing from a retail store will get you arrested in a heartbeat; however, there are no payroll police.

An employer cannot call 911 and report the gossip at the coffeepot, so it just happens. Sure, neglect your job long enough and you'll eventually lose it, but there is no fear of going to jail, so it doesn't seem as bad.

Most wouldn't dare to take another's life regardless of the situation because of the stiff legal penalties associated with murder. However, many of those same folks don't think twice about harboring resentment and hatred toward someone who has caused them pain. Murder will get you locked up; hatred, well... if it's for a generally accepted "good reason," it is embraced as normal and a valid defense mechanism.

Who cares what the legal ramifications are? Look at this spiritually. As 1 John 3:15 states, *"Anyone who hates a brother or sister is a murderer, and you know very well that eternal life and murder don't go together"* (MSG).

We have allowed certain sins to become more acceptable than others. Both you and I are guilty of violating the *whole* law, and therefore, we need forgiveness and restoration from being equal to the worse sinner this world has ever encountered. If you grasp this reality, like the woman in the parable, your ability to love will be off the charts, enabling you to fulfill the commands of Christ easily.

Jesus said to him, "'You shall love the Lord your God with all your heart, and with all your soul, and with all your mind.' This is the greatest and first commandment. And a second is like it: 'You shall love your neighbor as yourself.' On these two commandments hang all the Law and the Prophets."
—Matthew 22:37–40

A Beautiful Balance

I believe that the body of Christ would be much more powerful if we could come to a unified conclusion on the debate between legalism versus grace. These opposing mindsets feed double-mindedness and wreak havoc on believers.

The two positions may be summarized briefly as follows: Legalism forces a set of rules, while grace, when it is taken too far, can issue license to sin. Legalism says you must perform; grace says performance is meaningless. Legalism argues for keeping every letter of the law. Grace claims that Jesus fulfilled the law and through His finished work, we are all set.

I believe both sides of the debate have taken their position too far and biblical truth should temper both approaches. We cannot earn our salvation, and the only way to fulfill the law is to be rooted and grounded in love. Holding both to the law *and* to grace brings balance, peace, joy, hope, and selfless action. We are saved by the work of Christ, and we obey out of an overflowing sense of love and gratitude.

Through Christ, you can keep the royal law. Accept God's grace, which enables you to do what you could never do on your own: love God and your neighbor. Romans 13:14 tells us to *"put on the Lord Jesus Christ, and make no provision for the flesh, to fulfill its lusts."* Likewise, Romans 13:12 says, *"Therefore let us cast off the works of darkness, and let us put on the armor of light."* Put on His armor daily as you strive to keep evil at bay and purge all wrongdoing from your life—the "big" stuff as well as the "little" stuff.

Remember, law and grace are not separate sides of the same coin. They are meant to be unified in one glorious whole. Pursue both and you will free yourself of double-minded sin.

WORKBOOK

Chapter Five Questions

Question: Do you sometimes compare your sins to those of others and feel like you are doing pretty well? Are you guilty of being self-righteous and judging others—and if so, what can you do to change this?

_____

_____

_____

_____

_____

_____

_____

_____

_____

_____

_____

Question: What did Jesus mean when He said, *"Do not think that I came to destroy the Law or the Prophets. I did not come to destroy, but to fulfill"* (Matthew 5:17)?

_____

_____

_____

_____

_____

_____

_____

_____

_____

_____

Question: What is the difference between legalism and grace? How do the conclusions of this chapter challenge your views on the significance of God's law and His grace?

_____

_____

_____

_____

_____

_____

_____

_____

_____

_____

_____

Action: Reflect on the cross and the magnitude of what Jesus has done for you. Pray for God to reveal the depth of your sin to you—but rather than letting it discourage you, turn to Him in worship. Make a list of ways in which you can show love to your neighbor in light of the sacrificial love Christ has shown you.

_____

_____

_____

_____

_____

_____

_____

_____

_____

_____

Chapter Five Notes

CHAPTER SIX

A Double-Minded Belief

For a long time, I was bothered by a story in the Bible. Mark 9:14–29 tells of a father bringing an epileptic child, who had a deaf and dumb spirit, to Jesus. The father implored, "*Lord, I believe; help my unbelief*" (Mark 9:24).

This statement got to me. It challenged my belief, at the time, that a true follower should be all-in, doubting nothing. But rather than rebuke the man for his doubts, Jesus did exactly what the man had asked Him to do!

For years I struggled with this scripture because it didn't appear to align with other scriptures, like James 1:6a ("*But let him ask in faith, with no doubting*"), Mark 11:23 ("*whoever says to this mountain, 'Be removed and be cast into the sea,' and does not doubt in his heart, but believes that those things he says will be done, he will have whatever he says*"), or Matthew 21:22 ("*And whatever things you ask in prayer, believing, you will receive.*")

How could Jesus reward unbelief?

God eventually showed me a valuable truth: the fact that the devil is planting seeds of doubt in your mind doesn't mean you are double-minded. The voice telling you that you'll never hear from God, that He will never bless you with a job, that you'll never find the right spouse—the voice that constantly brings up your past failures—does not make you double-minded in and of itself.

However, allowing that voice to take root in your heart does.

A Father's Love

Let's go through the passage in Mark slowly to catch all of the salient points.

Mark 9:14–16 begins the story:

> *And when He came to the disciples, He saw a great multitude around them, and the scribes disputing with them. Immediately, when they saw Him, all the people were greatly amazed, and running to Him, greeted Him. And He asked the scribes, "What are you discussing with them?"*

Jesus could probably sense the tension and lack of faith among them. The scribes were taunting the disciples because they couldn't get the job done and heal the boy. The disciples had no idea what was going on, and doubt had crept in because of the boy's horrific condition.

Then someone in the crowd answered and said:

Teacher, I brought You my son, who has a mute spirit.
And wherever it seizes him, it throws him down; he
foams at the mouth, gnashes his teeth, and becomes
rigid. So I spoke to Your disciples, that they should
cast it out, but they could not.

—Mark 9:17–18

The boy's father popped out from among the crowd, jumped right into the middle of a question Jesus posed to the scribes, and purposely cut them off from speaking any more words of doubt. Clearly, the situation looked grim, but this man's faith moved him to trust Jesus anyway: "*I brought you my son....*" He had already asked the disciples for help, without success. Yet, while I'm sure he was disappointed, his faith had not wavered. He still believed Jesus held the answer.

Jesus had rather harsh words for those present: "*He answered him and said, 'O faithless generation, how long shall I be with you? How long shall I bear with you? Bring him to Me*'" (Mark 9:19).

Here, Jesus was lamenting how far His followers still had to go on their journey to knowing and living with God. He was basically saying, "How long do I have to put up with you in your unbelief? What is it going to take for you to believe with the eyes of your heart and not the eyes in your head?"

Then they brought him to Him. And when he saw Him,
immediately the spirit convulsed him, and he fell on
the ground and wallowed, foaming at the mouth. So
He asked his father, "How long has this been happen-
ing to him?" And he said, "From childhood. And often

> *he has thrown him both into the fire and into water to destroy him."*
>
> **—Mark 9:20-22a**

Can you imagine watching your child suffer so wretchedly for so long? The father's mind was filled with years of tormented memories. And I'm sure the child's condition seemed irreversible by all human standards. Many of us today go through far less and have lost hope and faith as a result, but not this man. This father remained undeterred in his course of action, regardless of what he had experienced.

> *But if You can do anything, have compassion on us and help us.*
>
> **—Mark 9:22b**

I believe with all my heart that this guy knew Jesus was capable yet could not perform mighty works in the midst of so much unbelief. Mark 6:5 states, *"Now He could do no mighty works there, except that He laid His hands on a few sick people and healed them."* This was clearly a case for a mighty work, not just curing a common cold. The father knew in his heart that all of the unbelief surrounding them could have prevented Christ from performing this miracle, which is why he said *"if you can,"* not knowing for sure.

Could the current atmosphere of unbelief and doubt block the power of God?

Jesus responded to the man, "*If you can believe, all things are possible to him who believes*" (Mark 9:23). Seeing his faith, Jesus immediately turned the table back on the man by saying that "*if* you can believe, all things are *possible*." And at once, "*the father of the child cried out and said with tears, 'Lord, I believe; help my unbelief!'*" (Mark 9:24).

The father immediately cried out in faith, without regard to any of his surroundings! An amazing and very dramatic transformation had just happened in the spirit of the father. When he first addressed Jesus, he had called Him "*Teacher*," but when he cried out this last time, he called Jesus "*Lord*."

The Greek word for *teacher* is *didaskalos*, which means an instructor or "one who teaches concerning the things of God."[7] The Greek word for *Lord* is *kyrios*, which means "supreme in authority," "controller," or "master."[8] This man went from merely wanting to get something from Jesus to surrendering fully to Jesus and giving Him something of great value: himself. Understanding the vast difference is critical!

The presence and calmness of Christ in the face of this adversity boosted the father's belief and commanded his heart to stand firm. His tears reflected the burden of caring for the boy—the crazy, demanding, exhausting way they had to live was all proof that he, too, needed healing from the tattered ruins of his mind plagued with the devil's lies, which is why, in verse 22, he implored Jesus, "*Have compassion on us*."

Most people today think that the father was lacking in faith. However, it is clear that the father believed his son could be healed, and he showed his faith through his actions. He brought his son out into the dusty streets in this awful condition, not knowing how long it would take to get to Jesus. He saw the disciples healing others but not his son. He waited.

He waited for the Healer Himself, without regard for the onlookers' ridicule and derision. He cut right into the middle of a conversation between Jesus and the religious leaders, jumping over the heads of the disciples. His faith and passion rose to the occasion. This was a man on a mission. He was not going to quit until he got what he wanted, which he did:

> *When Jesus saw that the people came running together, He rebuked the unclean spirit, saying to it: "Deaf and dumb spirit, I command you, come out of him and enter him no more!" Then the spirit cried out, convulsed him greatly, and came out of him. And he became as one dead, so that many said, "He is dead." But Jesus took him by the hand and lifted him up, and he arose.*
>
> **—Mark 9:25–27**

The devil was mad, and for a moment the condition looked worse—but only for a moment. If you pray for deliverance and see the situation go in the wrong direction, don't retreat. Believe in what the Bible promises, not in what you see! This biblical account serves as a reminder to consider the spiritual side of illness, rather than focusing merely on its physical nature. Let us not forget about the power of prayer when dealing with health issues.

Later, the disciples asked Jesus why they had failed to heal the child (Mark 9:28).

So He said to them, "This kind can come out by nothing but prayer and fasting."

—Mark 9:29

"*This kind*" referred to the unbelief, not to the foul, dumb, deaf spirit. The prayer and fasting needed to come before the attempt to cast out something as powerful as unbelief.

Battling Unbelief

James 4:7 says, "*Therefore submit to God. Resist the devil and he **will** flee from you*" (emphasis mine). It doesn't say, after you submit, to pray and fast. No, true submission is in the heart. When you submit to the Lordship of Jesus Christ, you can instantly see the results Jesus produces.

Unbelief or doubt in your heart is not good. Your mind is a battlefield where all things good and evil are conceived. It is up to you to cast down ungodly imaginations. It's up to you to take every evil thought captive:

For though we live in the world, we do not wage war as the world does. The weapons we fight with are not the weapons of the world. On the contrary, they have divine power to demolish strongholds. We demolish arguments and every pretension that sets itself up

against the knowledge of God, and we take captive
every thought to make it obedient to Christ.
            —2 Corinthians 10:3–5 *(NIV)*

Through Christ, you have the ability to destroy negative thoughts. You can pull down the walls built up around your heart that keep you in bondage and rob you of peace and joy. You can lead all negative, un-Christlike thoughts out of your life so they don't have the ability to make it to your heart.

It's not a matter of eliminating *some* bad thoughts, but *all* of them. The Bible says to take "*every thought*" captive. When you experience doubt, fear, disbelief, or anything else that doesn't align with the life-giving, all-powerful Word of God, it is a thought planted by the enemy. Do not believe it for one second; it does not align with Scripture, and therefore, it is completely untrue, regardless of the circumstances.

You might not really understand what it means to bring every thought into captivity or make it a daily priority. You may have been conditioned to think that bad thoughts are normal, and in a way that voice of temptation *is* normal—but what you do with that voice makes all the difference in the world.

A Constant Battle

Spiritual battles are ongoing. Demonic forces don't shut down and go to bed at night when you do. You are at war whether you realize it or not. You have to fight all the days of your life whether you like it or not. Doing nothing is doing something.

This is one of the many reasons why we should be infuriated with this fallen world. Paul said, in Ephesians 4:26, to "*be angry, and do not sin*," and he continued, "*Do not let the sun go down on your wrath*."

For years I have heard it said, and believed, that it is okay to be angry during the day but, by golly, you'd better not to go to bed mad. Today, I am fully convinced that we are to acquire a righteous anger regarding sin and its adverse effects on our lives—and then hold on to this newfound anger 24/7, 365 days a year. Paul said, "*Do not let the sun go down on your wrath*," meaning you should cling to that anger whether the sun is up or the sun is down. Do not let the sun going down cause you to lose sight of it.

One way to fight the good fight is as Paul instructed in Philippians 4:6–8 (NIV):

> *Do not be anxious about anything, but in every situation, by prayer and petition, with thanksgiving, present your requests to God. And the peace of God, which transcends all understanding, will guard your hearts and your minds in Christ Jesus. Finally, brothers and sisters, whatever is true, whatever is noble, whatever is right, whatever is pure, whatever is lovely, whatever is admirable—if anything is excellent or praiseworthy—think about such things.*

Your overall long-term well-being is very much dependent upon your beliefs. Your beliefs are a byproduct of your thoughts, and your thoughts control your life.

For example, every negative, scary, un-Christlike thought impacts your emotions; your emotions then influence your choices; and your choices then dictate the outcome of the actions in your life—or as the Bible would say, the *"fruit,"* whether good or bad. And by your fruit, you'll exude recognizable traits, whether as a child of God or a child of the devil (1 John 3:10).

You have a choice as to what gets meditated on: the fact that a thought enters your mind doesn't mean you have to entertain it. Through practice and wisdom, you can train yourself to make quick decisions about each thought that arises, whether to keep it or toss it out of your life, to your benefit.

God doesn't want us to live with unbelief. He understands the struggles of being human because He *"was in all points tempted as we are, yet without sin"* (Hebrews 4:15). Therefore, He has made a path to victory for us. Take it!

WORKBOOK

Chapter Six Questions

Question: How did the father of the boy demonstrate his single-minded faith through his actions?

_____

_____

_____

_____

_____

_____

_____

_____

_____

_____

_____

Question: What are some areas in which faith and doubt are wrestling for preeminence in your heart? What is the danger of allowing thoughts of unbelief to hold a place in your heart?

_____

_____

_____

_____

_____

_____

_____

_____

_____

_____

_____

Question: How can you "*take captive every thought*"?

_____

_____

_____

_____

_____

_____

_____

_____

_____

_____

_____

_____

Action: Read about the spiritual disciplines of prayer and fasting. Set aside a day this week for those purposes. Pray and fast specifically about any areas of unbelief in your heart.

Chapter Six Notes

CHAPTER SEVEN

Double-Minded Faith

You try to be a good Christian. You go to church. You tithe. You avoid profanity and excess alcohol. You do your morning devotions and nightly prayers. You check all the boxes you think are the most important.

But God yearns for something more from you.

James 2:19 states, "*You say you have faith, for you believe that there is one God. Good for you! Even the demons believe this, and they tremble in terror*" (NLT).

There is no doubt you can believe in God, knowing in your heart that there is a Creator and that there is way more to this life than the eyes can see, yet stop short of loving or fearing Him. Faith in God is much more than just believing He exists.

Unfortunately, most Christians today find themselves at a crossroads of believing they have faith while being completely void of the life-giving action that corresponds to genuine faith and produces biblical results. Paul described this as "*having a form of godliness but denying its power*" (2 Timothy 3:5a).

What good is believing in God if it doesn't change you or motivate you to do something about it? What good is going through the motions if you do not impact the world around you with your faith? Wavering in your belief in God is not double-minded faith. Rather, double-minded faith is failing to confirm your belief in God with corresponding action or works.

The Amplified Bible (AMP) continues in James 2:20 with these words: *"But are you willing to recognize, you foolish [spiritually shallow] person, that faith without [good] works is useless?"*

James asked in verse 14, *"What good is it, my brothers and sisters, if someone claims to have faith but has no deeds? Can such faith save them?"* The implied answer is *no!* To prove this beyond argument, he continued:

> Suppose a brother or sister is without clothes and daily food. If one of you says to them, "Go in peace; keep warm and well fed," but does nothing about their physical needs, what good is that? In the same way, faith by itself, if it is not accompanied by action, is dead.
> —*James 2:15–17 (NIV)*

Again, I ask the question: What good is believing in God if it doesn't motivate you to do something about it? You know exactly what James was talking about. Most of us feel compassion for others, but we don't take time out of our busy schedules to do something about it. We might send a card or a Facebook message saying we're praying for you, but do we really take the time to cry out to God on their behalf? Do we carry their burden as if it were our own? Are we willing to get in the trenches of life with those whom God has put in our path? Are we really loving our neighbors as ourselves?

Doers of the Word

James highlighted the example of Abraham:

> *You foolish person, do you want evidence that faith without deeds is useless? Was not our father Abraham considered righteous for what he did when he offered his son Isaac on the altar? You see that his faith and his actions were working together, and his faith was made complete by what he did. And the scripture was fulfilled that says, "Abraham believed God, and it was credited to him as righteousness," and he was called God's friend. You see that a person is considered righteous **by what they do and not by faith alone**.*
>
> **—James 2:20–24** *(NIV, emphasis mine)*

By faith, Abraham went when God called him to go. By faith, he stayed years in foreign countries, waiting on God to take him to the land He promised. By faith, he offered to sacrifice Isaac after waiting decades for his wife to bear a son. Abraham obeyed and was blessed.

John repeated this theme of God yearning for followers who would do His will:

> *But whoso hath this world's good, and seeth his brother have need, and shutteth up his bowels of compassion from him, how dwelleth the love of God*

in him? My little children, let us not love in word, nei-
ther in tongue; but in deed and truth. ... And
whatsoever we ask, we receive from Him, because we
keep his commandments, and do those things that
are pleasing in his sight.

—1 John 3:17–18, 22 *(KJV)*

Jesus clearly communicated in John 14:15–15:17 that
those who love Him will keep and obey His commandments. Moreover, those in Him bearing good fruit could
ask the Father anything in His name and it would be given:
"*If you ask anything in My name, I will do it*" (John 14:14).

Dare You To Move

There is a direct connection between faith and action.
Faith alone does not help you receive what you need from
God without the quickening of good works. Jesus had extreme words of judgment for those who did not follow the
royal law of love. Let us take a second look at Matthew
25:41–46:

"Depart from Me, you cursed, into the everlasting fire
prepared for the devil and his angels: for I was hun-
gry and you gave Me no food; I was thirsty and you
gave Me no drink; I was a stranger and you did not
take Me in, naked and you did not clothe Me, sick and
in prison and you did not visit Me."

Then they also will answer Him, saying, "Lord, when
did we see You hungry or thirsty or a stranger or na-
ked or sick or in prison, and did not minister to You?"
Then He will answer them, saying, "Assuredly, I say to

you, inasmuch as you did not do it to one of the least of these, you did not do it to Me." And these will go away into everlasting punishment, but the righteous into eternal life.

This may be a rude awakening for you. You may have thought that going to church and trying to be good was enough to please God. But as James said, *"For as the body without the spirit is dead, so faith without works is dead also"* (James 2:26).

Your good works ascend to God as a sweet aroma, *"the fragrance of Christ"* (2 Corinthians 2:15). By contrast, your dead faith simply stinks. It is death versus life—so choose life!

You can put in your time until you die, hoping for the best, or you can live a vibrant life pleasing to God. You can go through the motions and check the boxes, or you can dare to step out and *do the work* of the Father.

Don't carry the weight of a dead faith. Pour out the exquisite fragrance of your life in serving others. Help that family in need. Spend time with that depressed friend in your life. Go out and feed the hungry, clothe the naked, house the homeless, provide hope to the brokenhearted. When God says to go, *go.* Do. Love. Serve. It will cleanse your life of double-minded faith.

Let your light so shine before men, that they may see your good works, and glorify your Father which is in Heaven.
—Matthew 5:16 *(KJV)*

WORKBOOK

Chapter Seven Questions

Question: What are the types of works (actions or behaviors) typically associated with being a "good Christian"? How do these compare with the works that God values?

_____

_____

_____

_____

_____

_____

_____

_____

_____

_____

_____

Question: What are ways you can incorporate ministry to those in need into the relationships that are already part of your daily responsibilities as a spouse, parent, employee, etc. (e.g., helping a coworker, going as a family to minister)?

_____

_____

_____

_____

_____

_____

_____

_____

_____

_____

Question: Read Ephesians 2:10. Pray for God to lead you toward the specific good works that He has prepared for you. What did He impress upon your heart?

_____

_____

_____

_____

_____

_____

_____

_____

_____

_____

_____

Action: Looking through the book of James, as well as Matthew 25:31–46, make a list of the types of people whom believers are especially instructed to help. Next to each, write the names of people you know who are in that category. If you don't know of any individuals, write the names of organizations that help people in that situation. Plan a way that you can help in at least one ministry or help one individual starting this week.

_____

_____

_____

_____

_____

_____

_____

Chapter Seven Notes

_____

_____

_____

_____

_____

_____

_____

_____

_____

_____

_____

_____

_____

_____

_____

_____

_____

_____

_____

_____

_____

_____

CHAPTER EIGHT

Double-Minded Worldliness

Documented research has proven that just seven sources influence a person's thoughts and actions today: movies, television, music, family, books, law, and the internet. The same research shows that the local church has virtually no discernible influence on the lives of people.

- A Pew Research poll in 2010 found that Christians ranked only a small percentage higher than atheists in familiarity with the New Testament and with Jesus' teachings.[9]

- "Americans revere the Bible—but, by and large, they don't read it," wrote George Gallup Jr. and Jim Castelli, pollsters and researchers whose work focused on religion in the United States.[10]

- The Barna Group, a Christian polling firm, found in 2012 that Christians accepted the attitudes and beliefs of the Pharisees more than they accepted the teachings of Christ.[11]

- In 2013, Barna concluded that professional athletes have greater influence than professional clergy and faith leaders.[12]

- In 2015, a Pew poll showed nearly a 10 percent drop in Christianity over just the last seven years, with many on the verge of abandoning the faith. The writers stated, "They've drifted from a Bible-centered, Christ as God-centered faith, to a secularized, civil religion of ceremony and secularized liturgy."

  Furthermore, an emotional and politically correct Jesus "has replaced the actual Jesus who spent more time talking about hell than anyone else in the Bible and said He is the only and exclusive path to Heaven."[13]

No wonder our church leaders are growing weary. No wonder they are scrambling to find the latest and greatest message—some new revelation that no one's ever heard before. No wonder churches resemble rock concerts and entertainment centers. We use flattery to try to hold people in those pews as long as possible, because the church leaders see the writing on the wall—an evaporating Christian church.

No wonder we are catering to worldly desires instead of preaching a crucified, resurrected Christ and discipling people. No wonder we are focused more on entertainment than on one-on-one discipleship. No wonder we are double-minded when it comes to the world and our relationship with it.

And no wonder people are putting a fish magnet on their car and a cross around their neck before they have counted the cost of following Him (Luke 14:25–33). No wonder we have people calling themselves Christian when they know very little about what Christ taught.

Narrow Is the Gate

Jesus said to *"seek first the Kingdom of God"* (Matthew 6:33). Not movies, not actors, not sports, not even family—He said to seek God first and *then* you'll receive everything else you want in life.

But do we do this? Do we put our relationship with God first? Or do we tend to hold on to the things that we think will bring us safety, security, prosperity, success, or notoriety? Do we tend to be influenced the most by things that have nothing to do with our eternal salvation?

And, in turn, are we teaching new believers to do the same? Are we welcoming them into the fold by offering them terrible examples of what it means to live like Christ?

I've posed a lot of questions here, and they aren't easy to answer. But we are fooling ourselves if we believe we have things figured out.

It is difficult to know what's good and what's evil anymore—especially when we do such a poor job of teaching good and evil! The church is facing a crisis, which means you could be facing a crisis as well and not even realize it's happening.

Amidst all of this confusion, how can you avoid the trap of being double-minded? How can you coexist with a world that has it all wrong—even in many churches?

Friendship with the World

Let's compare three different translations of James 4:4:

Adulterers and adulteresses! Do you not know that friendship with the world is enmity with God? Whoever therefore wants to be a friend of the world makes himself an enemy of God. (NKJV)

You adulteresses [disloyal sinners—flirting with the world and breaking your vow to God]! Do you not know that being the world's friend [that is, loving the things of the world] is being God's enemy? So whoever chooses to be a friend of the world makes himself an enemy of God. (AMP)

You're cheating on God. If all you want is your own way, flirting with the world every chance you get, you end up enemies of God and his way. And do you suppose God doesn't care? The proverb has it that "he's a fiercely jealous lover." (MSG)

The Bible is clear: the world is a dangerous friend. The thought of becoming an enemy of God pierces my heart. How foolish could we be? Yet Scripture makes it plain that if *you* choose to be a friend of the world, *you* take a stand as an enemy of God.

The issue is that over time, *"all that is in the world— the lust of the flesh, the lust of the eyes, and the pride of life"* (1 John 2:16) leads most people to a slow, subtle death.

Paul wrote in his letter to Timothy that despite all he endured for his faith, it was going to be harder to be a Christian further down the road because *"men shall be lovers of their own selves, covetous, boasters, proud, blasphemers, disobedient to parents, unthankful, unholy, without natural affection, trucebreakers, false accusers, incontinent, fierce, despisers of those that are good, traitors, heady, highminded, lovers of pleasures more than lovers of God"* (2 Timothy 3:2–4 KJV).

> *We know that we have come to know him if we keep his commands. Whoever says, "I know him," but does not do what he commands is a liar, and the truth is not in that person. But if anyone obeys his word, love for God is truly made complete in them. This is how we know we are in him: whoever claims to live in him must live as Jesus did.*
> **—1 John 2:3–6** *(NIV)*

"In Him" is separation from the world. If you keep His commands continually, you distinctly differentiate yourself from most peers, colleagues, family, and friends. First John 2:15–16 adds:

Do not love the world or the things in the world. If anyone loves the world, the love of the Father is not in him. For all that is in the world—the lust of the flesh, the lust of the eyes, and the pride of life—is not of the Father but is of the world.

According to this scripture, there are three areas that indicate when someone is far too friendly with the ways of the world:

Lust of the flesh. This is slothfulness, laziness, hatred, illicit sex, idolatry, greed, strife, food cravings, selfishness, and self-preservation. It is when someone's main focus is on meeting the needs of the flesh and giving in to that human temptation.

Lust of the eyes. This is the desire to possess what we see or to have those things which whet our visual appetite. It is a lust for things like unmarried sexual relations or material possessions.

Pride of life. This boils down to a desire to be known and to have the good opinion of others. It's a yearning for recognition, status, and power. *Pride of life* includes anything that leads to arrogance, pride, presumption, and boasting.

Set Apart

Rather than remain set on worldly desires that will fail and leave you wanting more, your heart and mind should be set on God. First John 2:17 tells us, "*And the world is passing away, and the lust of it; but he who does the will of God abides forever.*"

You must focus your attention on those things pleasing to God, not on those things that please your selfish, worldly desires. Think about it: Would you prefer momentary pleasure on earth or eternal life in heaven? The choice couldn't be much clearer.

> *I beseech you therefore, brethren, by the mercies of God, that you present your bodies a living sacrifice, holy, acceptable to God, which is your reasonable service. And do not be conformed to this world, but be transformed by the renewing of your mind, that you may prove what is that good and acceptable and perfect will of God.*
> **—Romans 12:1–2**

In Romans 12:9–21, Paul described what it means to present your body as a sacrifice:

- Love without hypocrisy.
- Hate all that is evil or contrary to God's Word.
- Cling to what is good.
- Be kindly affectionate to one another, preferring to give instead of receive.

- Don't be slothful (lazy) in business.
- Be fervent in the Spirit, serving the Lord.
- Be patient in tribulation.
- Continue steadfastly in prayer.
- Provide for the needs of the saints.
- Demonstrate hospitality (taking in and loving on strangers).
- Bless those who persecute you.
- Bear the burdens of others.
- Unite in the same mind with others.
- Humble yourself. Do not repay evil with evil.
- Only deal in honesty.
- Live peaceably with all men.
- Overcome evil with good.
- Allow only God to avenge you.

Live your life as a living sacrifice, focusing on holiness, and you will steer clear of worldliness. You will cling to Christ and truth. You will rise above double-mindedness as you exemplify one who is fully focused on God.

Different in a Good Way

If you research the early church, you will find that its members stood out. They did things differently from the rest of society, which consequently drew attention. Society knew they were different because of their joy and peace amid fierce persecution, because of their love for one another, and because of their devotion to Christ (Acts 4:13).

If you are not hated for your relentless pursuit of truth and selfless service to others, you may not be as free from the world as you should be. The Bible is crystal clear that *"you will be hated by all for My name's sake"* (Matthew 10:22, Mark 13:13) yet be blessed in the face of persecution. Folks will speak evil about you, spreading lies and even reviling your name, but such persecution is a testament to your faith and should be expected (Matthew 5:11 KJV).

Not only are you blessed, but you also ought to *"rejoice, and be exceedingly glad: for great is your reward in heaven"* (Matthew 5:12a KJV). Until I truly understood this verse, I lived to be liked and avoided any rocking of the boat. However, while seeking that worldly peace of being left alone and merely living life, I had no inner peace. Once I truly committed to following Christ and started actually obeying the Word, it didn't take long for persecution to come.

Hatred started hitting my inbox, and folks started making all sorts of negative comments about me on social media. This persecution showed me that I was now on the right road and this part of the Bible was coming true in my life. Without people hating me, spreading lies, and making false accusations, I wouldn't have the real-life, biblical proof that I was "in Him," and He was in me, doing good works.

Knowing Jesus and serving Him, and consequently making waves, should be the hallmark of our faith. We should stand out as people who passionately love, relentlessly serve, constantly give, and purposely build up others. Living in this manner is the most daring thing we can do in a world that wants nothing more than for us to feed our lusts and worry about ourselves.

Believe me, live God's way and people will hate you, persecute you, and revile your name. According to the Word of God, you cannot live a Christian life without taking this path.

WORKBOOK

Chapter Eight Questions

Question: What (or who) are the greatest influences in your life? Do they draw you closer to Christ or to the world?

_____

_____

_____

_____

_____

_____

_____

_____

_____

_____

_____

Question: What are some of the things churches do to attract and hold people? To what extent do you think these methods are encouraging Christlikeness versus worldliness? Why? How do the church growth methods you see compare to the early church and how it drew people?

_____

_____

_____

_____

_____

_____

_____

_____

_____

_____

_____

Question: What are indicators of a life submitted to God? Which items on the Romans 12 list reveal double-mindedness in your life?

_____

_____

_____

_____

_____

_____

_____

_____

_____

_____

_____

_____

Action: Look at the list of seven sources that most influence people. Ask the question: "How can I honor and grow closer to God through _____ [music, friends, etc.]?" Write out ways each source of influence can be a tool for godliness, and then enact changes where you have been double-minded. *(Use the following Chapter Eight Notes page for additional space.)*

_____

_____

_____

_____

_____

_____

_____

_____

Chapter Eight Notes

_____

_____

_____

_____

_____

_____

_____

_____

_____

_____

_____

_____

_____

_____

_____

_____

_____

_____

_____

_____

_____

_____

CHAPTER NINE

The Double-Minded Church: Division

Double-mindedness is not something that only plagues individual Christians—it plagues the church as a whole. And double-mindedness in the church is strongest in the area of division. On a personal level, this is similar to the issue of double-minded favoritism, but when it's implemented on a churchwide level, it assumes a much more dangerous form.

What Is Church?

To fully understand the problem of double-mindedness in the church, it is essential to clarify the definition of *church*. The Greek word *ekklesia* (*ek-klay-SEE-ah*) refers to church, churches, or an assembly. It occurs 118 times in the King James Version of the Bible.[14] It could mean for instance, a group of Christians assembled for worship, a self-governing group of Christians with a particular set of religious traditions, or the whole community of Christians dispersed throughout the earth.

Strong's Concordance defines *ekklesia* as "a calling out, (concretely) a popular meeting, especially a religious congregation (Jewish synagogue, or a Christian community of members on earth or saints in heaven or both)—assembly, church."[15]

As seen throughout Scripture, the Bible refers to the church as the whole body of believers under Christ's direction and leadership:

> *And he is the head of the body, the church.*
> **—Colossians 1:18a** *(NIV)*

> *For the husband is the head of the wife, as Christ also is the head of the church; and He is the Savior of the body.*
> **—Ephesians 5:23**

In essence, the church is a people, not any particular building or location. Church is not a place you go to—rather, you *are* the church! The church is the body of believers united together in the calling of our Lord and Savior Jesus Christ. Church is you and me—us—living in communion, or a community visibly seen and hated by the world because we thrive in a toxic environment, unaffected by the surrounding wickedness.

The church is one body of believers with one passion, doing His work, building each other up in love. Well, that's what it *should* be, anyway! When people come to church to be served and entertained, rather than to take ownership and seek to be the hands and feet of Christ, we are in trouble.

Body Unity

Today, most Christians really believe church is where they go to worship on Sunday. Take, for example, the terminology we use today surrounding church, at which most would just shrug their shoulders.

Most people say, "I am going to church." Doesn't this sound as if they think church is a place they go?

How about "I go to Pastor Doug's church"? Doesn't this make it seem as if the speaker believes Pastor Doug has a different church than Pastor Bob? If your mind is telling you they *are* different churches, this point I'm making is definitely for you!

Lastly, consider the statement, "I am a member of the Baptist church." Are the Baptists different from the Methodists, who are different from the Catholics, and so on? The answer is *yes*—the question is *why*?

I will tell you why. Someone at some point didn't get along with or see eye to eye with someone else, so a church split happened, a wedge was inserted, and the body was broken.

This type of dividing and subdividing of the body of Christ started in Paul's day. Paul warned about the double-minded division in the church. In his first letter to the Corinthians, he wrote:

Now I plead with you, brethren, by the name of our Lord Jesus Christ, that you all speak the same thing, and that there be no divisions among you, but that you be perfectly joined together in the same mind and in the same judgment. For it has been declared to me concerning you, my brethren, by those of Chloe's household, that there are contentions among you. Now I say this, that each of you says, "I am of Paul," or "I am of Apollos," or "I am of Cephas," or "I am of Christ." Is Christ Divided? Was Paul crucified for you? Or were you baptized in the name of Paul?"
—1 Corinthians 1:10–13

Paul wanted nothing to do with people picking sides, creating division, or separating because one preacher has better speaking skills over another, one building has better acoustics than the other, one pastor understands your needs better than the other—or any other reason known to man that gets offered as an excuse for divisiveness.

If Paul were to address us today, he might phrase it this way: "Each of you says, 'I am of Rome' (Catholic), 'I am of Luther,' or 'I am of Wesley.' But was John Wesley crucified for you? Were you baptized in the name of Luther?"

My point is, the denominational lines that have been drawn in the sand continue to bring division and double-mindedness to the body of Christ. This body is made up of many parts, neatly fit together, working in harmony for the use and betterment of the whole. As Paul explained:

The eye cannot say to the hand, "I have no need of you," nor again the head to the feet, "I have no need of you." But quite the contrary, the parts of the body that seem to be weaker are [absolutely] necessary; and as for those parts of the body which we consider less honorable, these we treat with greater honor; and our less presentable parts are treated with greater modesty, while our more presentable parts do not require it. But God has combined the [whole] body, giving greater honor to that part which lacks it, so that there would be no division or discord in the body [that is, lack of adaptation of the parts to each other], but that the parts may have the same concern for one another. And if one member suffers, all the parts share the suffering; if one member is honored, all rejoice with it.

Now you [collectively] are Christ's body, and individually [you are] members of it [each with his own special purpose and function].
—1 Corinthians 12:21–27 (AMP)

Paul used the human body as a metaphor for the church. Each part is critical to all the others.

For example, if you want to do something as easy as picking something up off the floor, you need the skeletal system to support the muscles, the nerves to receive the message from the brain, the heart to pump the blood, and the skin to hold it all together. It's a simple task, but if you take just one body part out of the equation, none of it works.

When one part of your physical body breaks down, it has an adverse effect on the rest. The same is true of the church. Each person is integral to the others, and the body of Christ only works properly in unity.

The body of Christ achieves its maximum potential when it is working as one. This is why division is one of the most dangerous problems the church can face.

The Effect of Division

The church is immersed in a boiling pot of division today, but few think anything about it. It is just the way things are—or so we think. Division has survived for generations, and we seem blind to the damage it does to the body of believers.

At the slightest hint of division among believers, Paul went bananas. Remember what he wrote in 1 Corinthians 1:12: *"Is Christ divided? Was Paul crucified for you? Or were you baptized in the name of Paul?"* No!

Back up to verse 10 and read: *"Now I plead with you, brethren, by the name of our Lord Jesus Christ, that you all speak the same thing, and that there be no divisions among you, but that you be perfectly joined together in the same mind and in the same judgment."*

Fast-forward some 1,500 years and you find Catholics, Lutherans, Calvinists, Methodists, Baptists, Seventh-day Adventists, Episcopalians, Wesleyans, Presbyterians, and the list goes on and on and on. In my research, I discovered that nearly every one of the denominations was started by a single person who either split from another denomination or was kicked out of the church.

The Protestant Reformation in 1517 caused what looks like the largest church split in history. Martin Luther, a Catholic monk, wrote a proclamation of ninety-five theses regarding the need for reform in the Church. Luther was ultimately removed from the Roman Catholic Church following this critique. It is estimated that there are thousands of different Protestant denominations today as a direct or indirect result of the division between Martin Luther and Rome.

John Calvin also participated in the Reformation, breaking from the Catholic Church in 1530. He authored the doctrine of predestination, which holds that you are chosen to be saved or not saved—you have no choice. His followers are called Calvinists. Presbyterianism started in 1707, also based on the theology of John Calvin.

John Wesley was an Englishman who founded the Methodist Church. He began his ministry in the American colonies and then moved to London, where he joined the Moravian Christians. He disputed the theology of Calvin, embraced Arminian doctrines, and started the Methodist movement. The Wesleyan Church is also linked directly to John Wesley.

The Free Methodist Church was formed by Benjamin Titus Roberts, who was kicked out of the Methodist Church. "Free" was added to the name of the new denomination because back then, pews were commonly sold or rented.

In 1833, William Miller shared his belief that the second coming of Christ would occur roughly in 1843. He had spent years in the Baptist church, studying the prophecies of Daniel, especially Daniel 8:14, which talks about the 2,300-day cleansing. Miller calculated that Christ would return in approximately 1843. Though he was obviously proven wrong, the Advent Church, the Seventh-day Adventist Church, and the Jehovah's Witnesses were built around his teaching. Other sects developed with their own theories and new predictions. All failed, yet many followers remained convinced. And so, division spread.

The Episcopalian Church was organized after the American Revolution. Separating from the Church of England in 1789, Episcopalians and their Anglican counterparts have historically claimed to represent a path between Catholicism and Protestantism.

This is just a very small sample of the many divides and splits that have plagued the church and hurt the body of believers.

It's no wonder, looking at the thing we call "church" today, that the power described in the book of Acts is missing. It's no wonder prayers go unanswered.

A House Divided

What does God think about this denominational fragmentation? Scripture clearly indicates that He is opposed to such division:

> *Now I urge you, brethren, note those who cause divisions and offenses, contrary to the doctrine which you learned, and avoid them. For those who are such do not serve our Lord Jesus Christ, but their own belly, and by smooth words and flattering speech deceive the hearts of the simple.*
>
> *—Romans 16:17–18*

That they all may be one; as thou, Father, art in me,
and I in thee, that they also may be one in us: that the
world may believe that thou hast sent me.
—John 17:21 *(KJV)*

Make every effort to keep yourselves united in the
Spirit, binding yourselves together with peace. For
there is one body and one Spirit, just as you have been
called to one glorious hope for the future. There is one
Lord, one faith, one baptism, one God and Father of
all, who is over all, in all, and living through all.
—Ephesians 4:3–6 *(NLT)*

God cannot be happy with us. Sure, He still moves and works in and through the church, but imagine how different things would be if we were unified. Imagine what would happen if we were one body, working together, each doing his or her part!

I appeal to you brothers, by the name of our Lord Je-
sus Christ, that all of you agree, and that there be no
divisions among you, but that you be united in the
same mind and the same judgement.
—1 Corinthians 1:10 *(ESV)*

While we cannot change what has happened in the past, we can change how we move forward.

Common Attitudes

Take a look at the following attitudes about church and see where you fit:

- You may think your church is perfect and no change is needed.

- You may have no idea that anything is wrong as you go through the religious motions.

- You may know things aren't quite right, but because you are accustomed to religious ritualism, you continue to do the same things over and over, hoping something changes for the better soon.

- You may be getting angry at the fact that what you've been taught as truth isn't working. You may be on the verge of calling it quits, or you may have already left the faith, discouraged and disappointed.

- You may get so angry—or passionate—that you take time to evaluate the situation to find out where you are, who you are, and, most importantly, whose you are without being influenced from the outside.

If you do the latter, you will find answers that were never hidden, but were covered by the double-minded deception of division that has infiltrated the body of Christ over the last two thousand years. God is not more distant today than He was on the Day of Pentecost, when He poured out His Spirit (Acts 2). He is just buried under layers of religious hypocrisy.

Peel away those layers of man-made information locked in your mind. If you are not receiving from God, it's you, not Him. He has already provided everything you need for *"life and godliness"* (2 Peter 1:3). He is waiting patiently, jealously, to draw near to you.

Come Together

As you move toward unity in your life and with others, how do you maintain it long-term? How do you ensure that the snares of division and dissension don't undo what God will do and is already doing?

Be sure that what you hear, see, and believe aligns with Scripture. Set your heart on finding and living the truth, *"casting down arguments and every high thing that exalts itself against the knowledge of God, bringing every thought into captivity to the obedience of Christ"* (2 Corinthians 10:5). This will keep you in tune with the Spirit's leading.

It is vitally important that you test every thought to make sure it is in line with Scripture before you believe it. This means you will have to take the time to study your Bible, researching and meditating on Scripture. Living out the truth has to be your main priority in life, beyond the obligations of family, friends, work, and the concerns of daily life.

Submit to God. Knock and keep knocking; seek and keep seeking; ask and keep asking with a pure and humble heart (see Matthew 7:7). Every day acknowledge that He is the one in charge. This will prevent any divisions from entering your own heart.

Love God with all your heart, mind, soul, and strength and love your neighbor as yourself (Mark 12:30–31). Give up ulterior motives, self-preservation, backstabbing, strife, and envy. In short, love as Christ loved. This will also keep your heart free of division. When you live this way, you will promote unity in the church body as well.

Ask for wisdom to identify people who pose a threat to unity. Many Christians think you are supposed to embrace everyone under all circumstances, regardless of their condition, and accept them for who they are, even if they continue living in sin. That attitude is not scriptural. Unity in the body of Christ is for repentant, humble, God-fearing believers, not those who just claim to be Christians without submitting to the Lordship of Jesus.

The Bible talks about this numerous times. First, Jesus told the Pharisees, "*You are of your father the devil*" (John 8:44a). The Pharisees were the most religious, Bible-thumping group of the day, yet Jesus called them out as a threat to His kingdom! This shows that even the people who appear to have it all together can be a danger to unity.

Jesus also said, "*Do not think that I came to bring peace on earth. I did not come to bring peace but a sword. For I have come to 'set a man against his father, a daughter against her mother, and a daughter-in-law against her mother-in-law'* " (Matthew 10:34–35).

Later, Paul advised believers, *"Warn a divisive person once, and then warn them a second time. After that, have nothing to do with them. You may be sure that such people are warped and sinful; they are self-condemned"* (Titus 3:10–11 NIV).

Another example is found in 2 Thessalonians 3:14: *"Now if anyone [in the church] does not obey what we say in this letter, take special note of that person and do not associate with him, so that he will be ashamed and repent"* (AMP).

The verses quoted above do not contradict the message of unity. Rather, they indicate that biblical unity was for those who were obedient to the Word. If you did not obey, you were out of the Christ-centered circle.

Today, it is nearly impossible to hold to these biblical truths so that they bring forth the correction and repentance needed, because a person who is shunned by one church for not obeying the gospel will be welcomed by numerous other churches without any change in heart.

Selfishness, coupled with division, has crippled the body so severely that attempting to hold people responsible for their actions backfires. They simply go to a "different" church (as if there were such a thing), and they do it without shame or repentance. There are thousands of different church organizations, most with some sort of conflicting doctrine, all willing to take in someone who was kicked out of the church building down the street.

In order to unify individuals, it is necessary to divide them from others. For example, if I ask all members of a group who have blue eyes to stand up, I am unifying the blue-eyed people while simultaneously dividing them from the rest of the people, whose eyes have different colors. In the same vein, the Word of God should be dividing those who are being saved from those who are perishing.

In This Together

Division in the church carries its poison through generations, blinding us to the damage it inflicts to the body of Christ. No wonder prayers go unanswered! You can attend church your whole life but never experience true brotherhood or a life of love, unity, abundance, and blessings. You can go week after week, year after year, and become more discouraged as the cares of the world come at you in rapid-fire.

It's time for churches to throw off division. Come together and work toward unity! Let's reach across denominational lines and see past minor doctrinal differences. Let's put aside our divisive history and seek God above all else. Only then will our unity in Christ take root and flourish.

WORKBOOK

Chapter Nine Questions

Question: Why is division so dangerous for the church? What are some ways to avoid it?

_____

_____

_____

_____

_____

_____

_____

_____

_____

_____

_____

_____

Question: Give examples of when it would be right to separate from a church or denomination. If that does become necessary, with what attitudes should you depart?

_____

_____

_____

_____

_____

_____

_____

_____

_____

_____

_____

Question: Why is it so difficult to hold to biblical instructions about shunning a divisive person today? What are the results of this situation?

_____

_____

_____

_____

_____

_____

_____

_____

_____

_____

Action: Look at the list of common attitudes about the church. Think of someone you know who is affected by the first three. Begin a campaign of prayer for each of them. Ask the Lord for opportunities to talk to them about the truth of the Bible and who God is apart from false ideas they may have encountered in church settings.

Chapter Nine Notes

CHAPTER TEN

The Double-Minded Church: Legalism

On a personal level, the problem of double-minded legalism is similar to that of double-minded sin. But when it's handed down from a leadership position, the danger is far more potent.

Some things Paul writes are difficult to understand. Irresponsible people who don't know what they are talking about twist them every which way. They do it to the rest of the Scriptures, too, destroying themselves as they do it. But you, friends, are well-warned. Be on guard lest you lose your footings and get swept off your feet by these lawless and loose-talking teachers.

—2 Peter 3:16–17 (MSG)

We must use the Word, and the Word alone, to make the final determination on everything. That said, it is possible to twist Scripture and misinterpret it. Selectively using only certain, isolated verses, it is possible to make a case for just about anything, whether or not it is true. Taking Scripture out of context or only using part of it to prove a point opens the door to more division and double-mindedness, especially today, at a time when most professing Christians do not really know what the Word says.

Let me give you an example: How many of each animal did Noah take on the ark? If you thought to yourself "two," you're in agreement with the vast majority of Christians—which is my point exactly.

> *Take with you seven pairs of all clean animals, the male and its mate; and a pair of the animals that are not clean, the male and its mate; and seven pairs of the birds of the air also, male and female.*
> **—Genesis 7:2-3a** (NRSV)

The correct answer, then, is fourteen of all clean animals and two of all unclean animals. When was the last time you saw a depiction of Noah's ark with fourteen sheep? How about fourteen of any kind of bird?

As simplistic as this example may be, it's critical to realize that the common perception of what Scripture says is often wrong. This is concerning because common misperceptions are not limited to the number of animals on the ark—they may also pertain to more important details, regarding salvation and how to live godly lives.

Because biblical facts are not written on the hearts of most men today, it is easy to deceive them. Often, people listen to a speaker who tells a compelling story that sounds accurate because some biblical references are used. And without *"taking every thought captive to the obedience of Christ,"* the listeners allow that information, whether it is accurate, a half-truth, or a flat-out lie, to take root in their belief systems.

I suggest that you spend most of your Bible study time directly in the Word; then feel free to supplement your spiritual diet with a teacher or preacher of choice. No matter where the information is coming from, including this very book you are reading today, put the content through the filtration system of the Word of God. Ask God to reveal His truth in all areas.

Scripture is our ultimate authority on all things, and we must make sure that we comprehend and apply it appropriately rather than falling into legalism. Twisting Scriptures and practicing legalism go hand in hand because a legalistic person longs to uphold the illusion that he or she follows the law perfectly, which simply cannot be done.

The Fallacy of Legalism

One day I turned on my radio and caught a sermon about the Ten Commandments, including a long list of abominations from the Old Testament. The speaker quoted Scripture about what you could or could not eat. His premise was that if it was an abomination to God then, it must be an abomination now.

However, his focus was on the pig alone. He ignored the rest of the passage, which mentions bears, frogs, and shellfish as also being unclean. And he also didn't question why we aren't out in the fields catching and eating locusts, crickets, and grasshoppers, which were at that time clean and normal fare (Leviticus 11:22).

This is where holding tightly to legalism begins to break down. A legalistic person must either hold to all of the law, at all times and without exception, or he or she must pick and choose which of the laws to adhere to. Since it is impossible for a person to follow the law perfectly every day of his or her life (we are human, after all), then what ends up happening is exactly what happened on that radio program. The legalistic person chooses which part of the law to follow.

This is where double-mindedness sets in, as each person develops a strong opinion about certain parts of Scripture while ignoring the rest. In other words, they twist Scripture to meet their needs and agenda.

Clean and Unclean Food

The topic of unclean food is central to our discussion of legalism and the danger of having an unhealthy relationship with the law. Genesis 7:2 states, "*You shall take with you seven each of every clean animal, a male and his female; two each of animals that are unclean, a male and his female.*" This is the first record that shows a distinction or a difference between animals. It does not tell us which were clean and which were not.

I believe that somewhere between the fall of mankind and the great flood, the hardness of man's heart conceived uncleanness as part of people's desire to justify themselves. Prior to the fall, *"God saw everything that He had made, and indeed it was very good"* (Genesis 1:31). Some scholars think that such distinctions were based on conventional wisdom at the time as to what was edible and what wasn't. For example, today in the United States, you would not generally eat cats, dogs, mice, rats, weasels, or groundhogs. You do eat chicken, turkey, pheasant, and duck, but not ravens, buzzards, or bats. The origins of certain Old Testament restrictions could be similar in nature.

In Genesis 1:29–30, you'll find that God made man, beasts of the field, birds of the air, and all creatures that move along the ground to be vegetarians. The first time a mention of unclean animals was made wasn't until Genesis 7:2, but no specifics were recorded.

Then, in Genesis 9, God told Noah and his family, *"Every moving thing that lives shall be food for you; I give you everything, as I gave you the green plants and vegetables"* (Genesis 9:3 AMP). It wasn't until the Mosaic law that specific animals were documented as unclean (Leviticus 11).

How could this be? How could an animal go from clean to unclean and, in the New Testament, back to clean again?

The illogic of this development is what leads me to conclude that the answer lies in the hardness of man's heart. To me, the concept is not fundamentally different from Israel demanding a king and forsaking God in 1

Samuel 8. It's no different from Moses issuing a bill of divorce and Jesus having to clear up that mess in Mark 10:5–9.

Free from the Law

The law was the objective standard to measure transgressions. God gave mankind the law so sinners would know how sinful they really are and how far they deviate from God's standards. The law showed man how much he needed God because on his own, without some measure of grace, it was impossible to follow the law perfectly. According to Romans 5:13, sin was in the world prior to the law, but until the law was given, sin could not be specified or measured clearly.

In Galatians 3:19, Paul identified the purpose of the law: "*What purpose then does the law serve? It was added because of transgressions, till the Seed should come to whom the promise was made.*" From this scripture, we know that the law was not God's final answer. It was a temporary stopgap to rein people in.

In Galatians 3:21–25, Paul continued:

Is the law then against the promises of God? Certainly not! For if there had been a law given which could have given life, truly righteousness would have been by the law. But the Scripture has confined all under sin, that the promise by faith in Jesus Christ might be given to those who believe. But before faith came, we were kept under guard by the law, kept for the faith which would afterward be revealed. Therefore the law was our tutor to bring us to Christ, that we might be justified by faith. But after faith has come, we are no longer under a tutor.

Living, vibrant faith, coupled with your actions in Christ, releases you from the law of Moses and places you under the law of Christ—that's the message here! Spiritually speaking, you no longer have to worry about what you eat and whether or not you are following the law perfectly. You only need to focus on your faith.

Jesus emphasized this in Mark 7:14b–23, when He taught that eating unclean food is nothing compared to having an evil heart:

"Hear Me, everyone, and understand: There is nothing that enters a man from outside which can defile him; but the things which come out of him, those are the things that defile a man. If anyone has ears to hear, let him hear!"

When He had entered a house away from the crowd, His disciples asked Him concerning the parable. So He said to them, "Are you thus without understanding also? Do you not perceive that whatever enters a man from outside cannot defile him, because it does not enter his heart but his stomach, and is eliminated, thus purifying all foods?" And He said, "What comes out of a man, that defiles a man. For from within, out of the heart of men, proceed evil thoughts, adulteries, fornications, murders, thefts, covetousness, wickedness, deceit, lewdness, an evil eye, blasphemy, pride, foolishness. All these evil things come from within and defile a man."

If that isn't enough to convince you, Paul addressed how to relate to food in Romans 14:1–2. He began:

> *Receive one who is weak in the faith, but not to disputes over doubtful things. For one believes he may eat all things, but he who is weak eats only vegetables.*

Later in the chapter, Paul elaborated further:

> *I know and am convinced by the Lord Jesus that there is nothing unclean of itself; but to him who considers anything to be unclean, to him it is unclean. Yet if your brother is grieved because of your food, you are no longer walking in love. Do not destroy with your food the one for whom Christ died. Therefore do not let your good be spoken of as evil; for the kingdom of God is not eating and drinking, but righteousness and peace and joy in the Holy Spirit. For he who serves Christ in these things is acceptable to God and approved by men.*

> *Therefore let us pursue the things which make for peace and the things by which one may edify another. Do not destroy the work of God for the sake of food. All things indeed are pure, but it is evil for the man who eats with offense. It is good neither to eat meat nor drink wine nor do anything by which your brother stumbles or is offended or is made weak. Do you have faith? Have it to yourself before God. Happy is he who does not condemn himself in what he approves. But he who doubts is condemned if he eats, because he does not eat from faith; for whatever is not from faith is sin.*
>
> **—Romans 14:14–23**

There are two major things we can take away from this text. First, eat with faith, doubting nothing. If you believe a food item is clean and good based on the fact that your body is the temple of the Holy Spirit, it is clean. If you sense it is not good, then don't eat or drink it.

Second, in order to operate in love, which is the fulfillment of the law, you must, at all times, be cautious and courteous to those in your surroundings so you won't create an obstacle in their relationship with God. We are commanded to "*love our neighbor as ourselves*," and Romans 14:15 tells us we "*are no longer acting in love*" when those in our presence are caused to stumble by our actions.

Though I am free and belong to no one, I have made myself a slave to everyone, to win as many as possible. To the Jews I became like a Jew, to win the Jews. To those under the law I became like one under the law (though I myself am not under the law), so as to win those under the law. To those not having the law I became like one not having the law (though I am not free from God's law but am under Christ's law), so as to win those not having the law. To the weak I became weak, to win the weak. I have become all things to all people so that by all possible means I might save some. I do all this for the sake of the gospel, that I may share in its blessings.
—1 Corinthians 9:19–23 (NIV)

You can see now that in Christ, you are free from the law. The legalism of the Old Testament does not need to concern you—unless you are trying to hold to certain parts of it instead of trying to fulfill the whole of it through love. Those who focus on some of the old law while ignoring other parts are also ignoring this wonderful truth found in the New Testament: that God is more desirous of a pure heart than a pure stomach.

The Way of Christ

What a serious offense it is to misuse Scripture or to hold tightly to some parts of the Bible while ignoring or twisting others (Matthew 5:18)!

As a church, we must accept that there is no way a person can adhere to every single law perfectly for the rest of his or her life. That's why God sent Jesus—to take away the sin of the world (John 1:29).

We must also acknowledge that the Christian life is not about getting everything we want. It's not about comfort or an easy life. It's about following Christ no matter what, even if that means missing out on some of the luxuries the world offers.

The church would do well to purge double-minded teachings from its pulpit. Preach the whole truth, not only part of it, and know that God will fill in the blanks. We can't lie to people in order to get them to heaven.

WORKBOOK

Chapter Ten Questions

Question: What relationship does the Christian have with the Old Testament law? Why does a legalistic person end up picking and choosing only certain laws to obey?

_____

_____

_____

_____

_____

_____

_____

_____

_____

_____

_____

Question: Using the example of clean and unclean foods, how do preachers and Bible teachers sometimes twist Scripture to suit their own ends? How can you safeguard against making Scripture mean what you want it to mean instead of its true interpretation?

_____

_____

_____

_____

_____

_____

_____

_____

_____

_____

Question: What is the solution to the problem that none of us can adhere to every single law perfectly?

_____

_____

_____

_____

Action: What is a hard teaching of the Bible that you have trouble accepting? Take time to study it in depth as you pray for understanding. Look at the cultural context, the surrounding passages, and the meaning of the words in their original languages. Read other passages on the same topic and the commentaries from reliable Bible teachers.

Chapter Ten Notes

_____

_____

_____

_____

_____

_____

_____

_____

_____

_____

_____

_____

_____

_____

_____

_____

_____

_____

_____

_____

The Double-Minded Church: Grace

Jesus paid the price with a one-time final sacrifice for all sin, for all mankind, forever (Hebrews 10:12). Just as Adam introduced sin and separated man from God, Christ made one payment to remove sin and bring us back to God (Romans 5:12).

Therefore, sin is not the roadblock keeping you from God. Jesus removed that barrier, giving you the possibility of a one-on-one relationship with the Creator of the universe. He knows exactly how many hairs you have on your head (Matthew 10:30). He put every star in place and knows them by name (Psalm 147:4). Truly awesome!

Thank God for His grace. Without His grace, His mercy, and His long-suffering, we would all be toast. Grace supersedes sin. Paul wrote:

The law was brought in so that the trespass might in-crease. But where sin increased, grace increased all the more, so that, just as sin reigned in death, so also grace might reign through righteousness to bring eternal life through Jesus Christ our Lord.

—Romans 5:20–21 (NIV)

So, no matter what your background or how much you have sinned in the past, the grace of God is infinitely bigger. The problem comes when you camp on that verse as a license to sin or a license to be loose with your morals. This is the root of double-mindedness, as worldly ways begin to infiltrate your life.

Paul warned about this: "*What shall we say then? Shall we continue in sin that grace may abound? Certainly not! How shall we who died to sin live any longer in it?*" (Romans 6:1–2). Then he continued:

Therefore do not let sin reign in your mortal body, that you should obey it in its lusts. And do not present your members as instruments of unrighteousness to sin, but present yourselves to God as being alive from the dead, and your members as instruments of righteousness to God. For sin shall not have dominion over you, for you are not under law but under grace.

What then? Shall we sin because we are not under law but under grace? Certainly not! Do you not know that to whom you present yourselves slaves to obey, you are that one's slaves whom you obey, whether of sin leading to death, or of obedience leading to righteousness?

—Romans 6:12–16

Over the last forty to fifty years, grace has been per-verted in the church. Grace has become an excuse for our shortcomings and selfish sinfulness. Rather than hold peo-ple's feet to the fire with the fear of the Lord and hold them accountable for their actions, pastors would rather fill their auditoriums by speaking a message easier to hear. The following scripture from the Gospel of John might as well be describing our society today:

> *This is the crisis we're in: God-light streamed into the world, but men and women everywhere ran for the darkness. They went for the darkness because they were not really interested in pleasing God. Everyone who makes a practice of doing evil, addicted to denial and illusion, hates God-light and won't come near it, fearing a painful exposure.*
> *—John 3:19–21 (MSG)*

Today, the church as we know it looks more to the world than to the Word for guidance. It has adopted the world's view of success. Over time, the church has gone from messages about sin and repentance to ear-tickling messages about grace to fill the seats. This extreme and unbiblical view of grace is just as dangerous as extreme legalism, and it's equally guilty of contributing to divi-sions within the church.

Lies from the Pulpit

Some of the verses that I used in the last chapter to prove all meat was clean sometimes get used today to prove that *everything* is okay with God and to provide a justification for loose living. Anything short of the truth, even an half-truth, is a lie.

Lack of wisdom and understanding, deafness in the spiritual ear, hardness of the heart, and plain deception—all can lead to lies that pull you away from Christ.

Twisting Scripture in this way is a common practice in many of today's churches. Let's look at just a couple of verses that can be pulled out of the Bible and used from the pulpit in this manner.

I can do all things through Christ who strengthens me.
—Philippians 4:13

Sure you can, if you are in Christ and He is in you, according to John 15:4! Way too many people are led to believe Jesus will never leave them nor forsake them yet find themselves lost and alone—and wondering why. The message behind this verse is powerful and amazing; however, it only works when combined with a healthy, obedience-filled relationship.

For assuredly, I say to you, whoever says to this mountain, "Be removed and be cast into the sea," and does not doubt in his heart, but believes that those things he says will be done, he will have whatever he says.
—Mark 11:23

This passage is one that church leaders use to energize followers and get them to believe that anything is possible if you just speak faith-filled words. While I don't disagree that anything is possible with God, most people today are speaking these supposedly faith-filled words and it isn't working. As discouragement sets in, they are just told to stand their ground (see Ephesians 6:13–14). Honestly, there are people who have been standing and believing for years with no change to their situation.

The reality is, it may not have anything to do with your believing. Quite simply, it could be your lack of knowledge, or it may be that you are living in disobedience or unforgiveness. Perhaps you are not connected to the Vine, at all, and thus are not allowing the power of God to flow into and through you.

I know these may come across as tough words. However, the Bible tells us in 2 Corinthians 13:5, *"Examine yourselves, to see whether you are in the faith. Test yourselves. Or do you not realize this about yourselves, that Jesus Christ is in you?—unless indeed you fail to meet the test!"* (ESV).

We are to *"seek first the Kingdom of God"* (Matthew 6:33). We are to deny ourselves, take up our cross and follow Him (Matthew 16:24). The real question is: Are we really doing these things?

In each of the above instances, some believers are lying to themselves and to others when they take portions of Scripture and twist them into half-truths. Creating a half-truth or changing the Word of God into something it isn't is a lie. The following Bible verses reflect how God feels about lying.

Old Testament

He who works deceit shall not dwell within my house; he who tells lies shall not continue in my presence.
—Psalm 101:7

These six things the LORD hates, yes, seven are an abomination to Him: a proud look, a lying tongue, hands that shed innocent blood, a heart that devises wicked plans, feet that are swift in running to evil, a false witness who speaks lies, and one who sows discord among brethren.
—Proverbs 6:16–19

Lying lips are an abomination to the LORD, but those who deal truthfully are His delight.
—Proverbs 12:22

A false witness will not go unpunished, and he who speaks lies will not escape.
—Proverbs 19:5

New Testament

But those things which proceed out of the mouth come from the heart, and they defile a man. For out of the heart proceed evil thoughts, murders, adulteries, fornications, thefts, false witness, blasphemies.

These are the things which defile a man, but to eat with unwashed hands does not defile a man.

—Matthew 15:18–20

You are of your father the devil, and the desires of your father you want to do. He was a murderer from the beginning, and does not stand in the truth, because there is no truth in him. When he speaks a lie, he speaks from his own resources, for he is a liar and the father of it.

—John 8:44

Therefore, putting away lying, "Let each one of you speak truth with his neighbor," for we are members of one another.

—Ephesians 4:25

Do not lie to one another, since you have put off the old man with his deeds, and have put on the new man who is renewed in knowledge according to the image of Him who created him...

—Colossians 3:9–10

But the cowardly, unbelieving, abominable, murderers, sexually immoral, sorcerers, idolaters, and all liars shall have their part in the lake which burns with fire and brimstone, which is the second death.

—Revelation 21:8

God is truth, and He hates lies. The verses above show the serious nature of lying and the eternal consequences that a liar will have to face. Let us not mistakenly think that lying, especially about God's truth, is a harmless matter.

Toward Healthy Christianity

To that effect, the wisdom of the Word isn't a matter of outward display or feeling better about yourself. It's grounded in a healthy fear of God. It keeps you from doing bad things even when no one is looking and makes you do good without needing notice or reward:

For God will bring every work into judgment, including every secret thing, whether good or evil.
—Ecclesiastes 12:14

For nothing is secret that will not be revealed, nor anything hidden that will not be known and come to light.
—Luke 8:17

If we say that we have no sin, we deceive ourselves, and the truth is not in us. If we confess our sins, He is faithful and just to forgive us our sins and to cleanse us from all unrighteousness. If we say that we have not sinned, we make Him a liar, and His word is not in us.
—1 John 1:8–10

But before you can get to that point, you must acknowledge your sin and your need for a Savior. Sure, you'll mess up. We all do. But if your heart is in the right place—if you desire to please God and hate it when you fall short—then He is faithful and just to forgive (1 John 1:9).

"My little children, these things I write to you, so that you may not sin" (1 John 2:1a). Why did John write this letter? So that you might not sin. But if for some reason you do sin, *"we have an Advocate with the Father, Jesus Christ the righteous"* (1 John 2:1b).

> *We know that we have come to know him if we keep his commands. Whoever says, "I know him," but does not do what he commands is a liar, and the truth is not in that person. But if anyone obeys his word, love for God is truly made complete in them. This is how we know we are in him: Whoever claims to live in him must live as Jesus did.*
> *—1 John 2:3–6 (NIV)*

> *No one who lives in him keeps on sinning. No one who continues to sin has either seen him or known him. Dear children, do not let anyone lead you astray. The one who does what is right is righteous, just as he is righteous. The one who does what is sinful is of the devil, because the devil has been sinning from the beginning.*
> *—1 John 3:6–8a (NIV)*

Willfully sinning after knowing the truth leaves you alone with no hope. You know something is wrong, but it no longer bothers you, and you even defend your actions to save face. You would rather sin than risk shame. But the repercussions for this way of thinking are severe: a hardened, unrepentant heart will keep you out of heaven.

For if we sin willfully after we have received the knowledge of the truth, there no longer remains a sacrifice for sins, but a certain fearful expectation of judgment, and fiery indignation which will devour the adversaries. Anyone who has rejected Moses' law dies without mercy on the testimony of two or three witnesses. Of how much worse punishment, do you suppose, will he be thought worthy who has trampled the Son of God underfoot, counted the blood of the covenant by which he was sanctified a common thing, and insulted the Spirit of grace?

—Hebrews 10:26–29

If you count the blood of Christ as no big deal and insult the Spirit of grace by using it to live a selfish, worldly life of sin, then you take yourself out from under the sacrifice made. Then there are no other options. Christ was the final payment. You are left with spiritual death.

Therein lies the ultimate danger of living a double-minded life. Yet double-mindedness is rampant in the body of Christ!

If your heart is hard, you may lack wisdom and understanding of what the Bible teaches (James 1:5). Don't let someone else do all the work while you sit back and catch the highlights. Perfect church attendance doesn't save your soul. The Kingdom is a contact sport—so get out there and take it by force!

WORKBOOK

Chapter Eleven Questions

Question: What does it mean that God's grace is infinitely bigger than our sins? What does it mean to you personally?

_____

_____

_____

_____

_____

_____

_____

_____

_____

_____

_____

Question: How can grace become a license to sin? How has the message of grace been perverted in the church?

_____

_____

_____

_____

_____

_____

_____

_____

_____

_____

_____

Question: What is the end result of living with a hardened, unrepentant heart? What is the current attitude of your heart toward sin?

_____

_____

_____

_____

_____

_____

_____

_____

_____

_____

_____

_____

Action: Is there a secret sin in your life that you are hiding to save face? Reread Hebrews 10:26–29 and resolve to become single-minded in your pursuit of Christ. Make a list of practical steps you can take to do away with that secret sin. Consider seeking accountability from a pastor or a trusted fellow believer in Christ.

Chapter Eleven Notes

_____

_____

_____

_____

_____

_____

_____

_____

_____

_____

_____

_____

_____

_____

_____

_____

_____

_____

_____

_____

_____

CONCLUSION

The Single Solution

One of the most powerful things you can do to avoid double-mindedness is to pray. However, prayer is in danger of becoming double-minded when it is full of doubt, not in line with God's will, or driven by selfish motives.

Prayer is the very first area that James addressed as a potential double-mindedness problem—but I figured we'd save the best for last!

Take Action

Pray without doubt. James addressed his preeminent concern for your prayer life when he said that one who is unsure, uncertain, doubting, or indecisive in prayer is a double-minded man (James 1:6–8). Doubt in your communication with God pulls the power plug in your relationship with Him. So pray boldly!

But also pray in line with Scripture and God's promises—with humility, not to make a spectacle of yourself:

And when thou prayest, thou shalt not be as the hypocrites are: for they love to pray standing in the synagogues and in the corners of the streets, that they may be seen of men, Verily I say unto you, they have their reward. But thou, when thou prayest, enter into thy closet, and when thou hast shut thy door, pray to thy Father which is in secret; and thy Father which seeth in secret shall reward thee openly. But when ye pray, use not vain repetitions, as the heathen do: for they think that they shall be heard for their much speaking. Be not ye therefore like unto them: for your Father knoweth what things ye have need of, before ye ask him.

—Matthew 6:5–8 *(KJV)*

Pray in right relationship. Many people have no idea when or how to pray, and they are frustrated when their prayers seem unanswered. They tend to go into prayer-warrior mode only when they need something or when life isn't going as planned. This is like damage-control prayer!

How much better off would we be if we were communing with God day in and day out, regardless of how good or bad things were going in our lives?

*Rejoice always, **pray continually**, give thanks in all circumstances; for this is God's will for you in Christ Jesus.*

—1 Thessalonians 5:16–18 *(NIV, emphasis mine)*

Be anxious for nothing, but in everything by prayer and supplication, with thanksgiving, let your requests be made known to God.

—Philippians 4:6

Before seeking God for something, ask yourself the following questions to determine if your prayer will please Him:

1. Do you ask according to His will? First John 5:14 says, *"Now this is the confidence that we have in Him, that if we ask anything according to His will, He hears us."* If our prayer is according to His will, the Bible says He hears us. We can know that our request or prayer is in His will if it lines up with Scripture and with the promises God has made to us.

2. Do you keep His commandments? First John 3:22 says, *"And whatever we ask we receive from Him, because we keep His commandments and do those things that are pleasing in His sight."*

Jesus stressed the importance of obedience in John 15:9–11 (NIV):

> As the Father has loved me, so have I loved you. Now remain in my love. **If you keep my commands, you will remain in my love**, just as I have kept my Father's commands and remain in his love. I have told you this so that my joy may be in you and that your joy may be complete.

Jesus also said, in John 15:7, *"If you abide in Me, and My words abide in you, you will ask what you desire, and it shall be done for you."*

Again, this comes down to knowing Scripture and following the path that God has established in His Word for how we are to live our lives. Shortly before his crucifixion and resurrection, Jesus told his followers, *"This is my commandment, that you love one another as I have loved you"* (John 15:12). Recall also, *"love is the fulfilment of the law"* (Romans 13:10), so if you want your prayers answered, you must keep and obey His command to *"love your neighbor as yourself."*

3. Are your motives self-centered or God-centered?
James 4:3 tells us, *"You ask and do not receive, because you ask amiss, that you may spend it on your pleasures."* If your end goal is to glorify yourself or put yourself in a better position above others, then your prayer won't be pleasing to God.

The bottom line is that if you can answer *yes* to the first two questions and *God-centered* to the third, you will have no problem staying single-minded in prayer.

Double-Minded No More

Perhaps this is the first time you have looked at these areas of double-mindedness, or perhaps you have sensed for a while that these are areas that need to be closely monitored and watched. Wherever you are in your journey, today is the day to get serious about becoming single-minded for Christ. Prayer, fasting, seeking God, and reading the Bible are all tools that God has provided to help you in your quest for single-mindedness.

Choose today to get control of these areas in your life. It is absolutely possible to leave double-mindedness behind if you make God the sole focus of your life. He is the One who will help you leave that state of compromise and hypocrisy behind. If you completely surrender to Him in all areas of your life and are led by the Holy Spirit, you will be able to live the Christian life to the fullest. As Jesus promised, *"I have come that they may have life, and that they may have it more abundantly"* (John 10:10b).

As this book draws to a close, remember: you are just one single, solid, unwavering decision away from eliminating double-mindedness and living wholeheartedly for God.

REFERENCES

Notes

1. "Double-minded." *Merriam-Webster Dictionary.* https://www.merriam-webster.com/dictionary/double-minded.

2. Strong, James. "G1374 – dipsychos." *Strong's Exhaustive Concordance of the Bible.* Hunt & Eaton, New York, 1894. In *Blue Letter Bible.* https://www.blueletterbible.org/lang/lexicon/lexicon.cfm?Strongs=G1374&t=KJV.

3. Mackinnon, Sean P., Christian H. Jordan, and Anne E. Wilson. "Birds of a Feather Sit Together: Physical Similarity Predicts Seating Choice." *Personality and Social Psychology Bulletin* 37, no. 7 (April 2011), p. 879–892. https://doi.org/10.1177/0146167211402094.

4. "Favoritism." *Merriam-Webster's Learner's Dictionary.* http://www.learnersdictionary.com/definition/favoritism.

5. "Favoritism." *American Heritage Dictionary of the English Language.* 5th edition. Houghton Mifflin Harcourt Publishing Company, 2018. https://ahdictionary.com/word/search.html?q=favoritism.

6. "Prosopolempsia." *The NAS New Testament Greek Lexicon.* https://www.biblestudytools.com/lexicons/greek/nas/prosopolepsia.html.

7. Strong, James. "G1320 – didaskalos." *Strong's Exhaustive Concordance of the Bible.* Hunt & Eaton, New York, 1894. Quoted in *Blue Letter Bible.* https://www.blueletterbible.org/lang/lexicon/lexicon.cfm?t=kjv&strongs=g1320.

8. Strong, "G2962 – kyrios." https://www.blueletterbible.org/lang/lexicon/lexicon.cfm?t=kjv&strongs=g2962.

9. "U.S. Religious Knowledge Survey: Executive Summary." *Pew Research Center: Religion and Public Life.* September 28, 2010. http://www.pewforum.org/2010/09/28/u-s-religious-knowledge-survey.

10. Gallup, George, and Jim Castelli. Quoted in Albert Mohler, "The Scandal of Biblical Illiteracy: It's Our Problem," January 20, 2016. https://albertmohler.com/2016/01/20/the-scandal-of-biblical-illiteracy-its-our-problem-4.

11. "Christians: More Like Jesus or Pharisees?" *Barna Research Group.* June 3, 2013. https://www.barna.com/research/christians-more-like-jesus-or-pharisees.

12. "Athletes Influence Greater than Faith Leaders." *Barna Research Group.* April 10, 2013. https://www.barna.com/research/athletes-influence-greater-than-faith-leaders.

13. "America's Changing Religious Landscape." *Pew Research Center: Religion and Public Life.* May 12, 2015. http://www.pewforum.org/2015/05/12/americas-changing-religious-landscape.

14. Strong, "G1577 – ekklēsia." https://www.blueletterbible.org/lang/lexicon/lexicon.cfm?t=kjv&strongs=g1577.

15. Strong, "G1577 – ekklēsia."

About the Author

Born into a broken home on Detroit's southwest side, Tim lived through two decades of trials that resulted in debilitating fear and anxiety that nearly killed him.

Then, after Tim had spent thirty years running from God and thinking He was merely a "crutch" for weak-minded people, God showed up—and, in a moment, He radically changed everything.

The experience Tim had with God ten years ago has transformed his life forever and completely healed him of fear, doubt, stress, gut-wrenching (almost crippling) anxiety, and an enlarged, erratic heart. As a student of the

Word, he has graduated from two major Bible colleges and continues to dig deeper daily. Tim is continually driven by his encounter with the glory of God, which he longs to experience again.

By adhering to biblically based core values both personally and professionally, Tim continues to initiate movements of fellowship and goodwill that have spilled over into every area of his life. As a dedicated husband, daddy, grand-daddy, and businessman, he is setting a standard of teaching by example and by living in the Word.

His life is a classic rags-to-riches story that has inspired many. Tim's continued perseverance in honoring Scripture has led to the recognition of not one, but two of his companies by *Inc. Magazine* as numbering among the fastest-growing privately held companies in America. This includes seven-time Inc. 5000 Hall of Fame Honoree Top Flite Financial and 2018 first-time qualifier Three T's Properties.

Against numerous odds, Tim's God-given vision has progressively materialized into a reality of spiritual and professional accomplishment. He oversees the daily operations of several multi-million-dollar corporations, diligently helps people in need, and relentlessly pursues biblical truth.

Homeless Angels is a Christian-based outreach in Lansing, Michigan. We rebuild and restore faith in humanity through innovative ideas, programs, and events. Our main goal is to involve the community in real change for people who are homeless or at risk of homelessness.

Homeless Angels Programs:

- Homeless Angels Street Ministry
- Homes of Hope
- Community-Funded Hotel Program
- Little Angels Diaper Bank
- Send an Angel to Camp - Scholarship
- Free Street Store

Photo courtesy of Tom Stone

In 2016, there were 66,483 homeless people in Michigan. Families with children made up 43% of Michigan's homeless population. The group with the largest increase were seniors over 55; these numbers climbed from 7,282 in 2014 to 7,919 in 2016.

By becoming a Sleep Over Safety Partner, (S.O.S), you will be helping the Homeless Angels in our mission to provide assistance for the homeless and those in need during their time of crisis. Our organization does not receive government funding, so your partnership is critical to the care and well-being of those we serve.

Your partnership will include recognition on our website Donor Page, our quarterly newsletter showing your donation at work, and as a small thank you, you will receive your choice of an S.O.S. Partner window cling or bumper sticker.

Please reach out today and consider becoming a Homeless Angel S.O.S Partner.

f 🗗 📷 homelessangels.org

Made in the USA
Las Vegas, NV
22 June 2021

25218887R00095